Columbus Salley & Ronald Behm

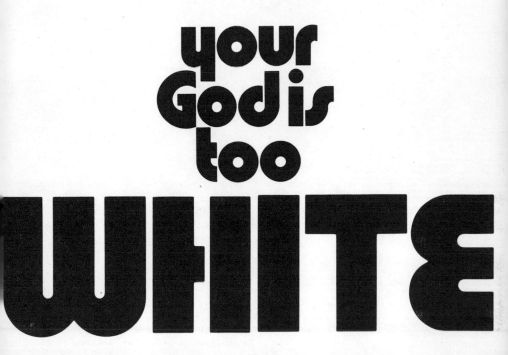

your God is too WHITE

Inter-Varsity Press
Downers Grove, Illinois 60515

© 1970 by Inter-Varsity Press

ISBN 0-87784-478-X
Library of Congress Catalog Card Number: 76-132957

Printed in the United States of America

dedication

to our wives:
Jacquelyn Salley and Barbara Behm
to our children:
Christopher and Jennifer Salley;
Herschel and Kurtis Jackson
and to my beautiful black mother
Vurnetha Donley who kept me alive

The white Jesus is dead. He was slain somewhere between Hiroshima or Nagasaki and the road to Selma, Alabama. And that Jesus will never be resurrected as the Christ. The book you are reading will tell you that he will remain forever entrapped amidst the images of pristinity which white middle-class America mistakes for purity.

Because the Jesus of Nazareth portrayed in America has been a minor part gospel and a major part Cotton Mather and Jonathan Edwards, we evangelicals have forgotten the essentially prophetic tradition and orientation out of which Jesus spoke. Revival, not revolution, has been the keystone to our understanding of the Kingdom. The Kingdom of God, however, is much more: *revival* and *revolution* met in a daily commitment to make straight in the deserts of our existence —deserts made by exploitive systems and barely subsistent life in ghettos—a highway "for our God."

Ronald Behm and Columbus Salley display a keen sensitivity to the Christ who was made man in order to serve. This was the Christ who reminded men of the Nazareths across from the opulence of Jerusalem. In other words, coming from the slums and ghettos he was seized by the Spirit and declared his anointment "to preach good news to the poor . . . to proclaim release to the captives and recovering of sight to the blind, to set at liberty those that are oppressed [some translations say, appropriately, "bruised"], to proclaim the acceptable year of the Lord."

Bros. Behm and Salley are to be commended for rejecting a "hear-no-evil, see-no-evil and speak-no-evil" type of pietism and for seeking active dialogue with those who are the victims of evil in its most heinous forms. Thus, these men are able to run to the militants (like Stokely Carmichael, Rap Brown and Malcolm X) rather than run away from them. The faith which they affirm is the substance of things hoped for —by the militants too—and Ron and Columbus are not afraid of seeing through and in the radical rhetoric traces of the prophetic abrasiveness of men like Amos and Hosea, Micah and Daniel.

Both men challenge white Christianity to take the crosses from their necks and their rostrum designs and put them on their backs in a common struggle to make this fractured nation a human community.

This book makes it obvious that they are not rejecting the Bible but are reconnecting the Bible to the events that take place on 43rd Street in Chicago, on 135th Street in Harlem, on High Street in Newark and on Union Avenue in Montgomery. Karl Barth once noted that one must read his Bible with his newspaper—or, if you will, the latest OEO profiles and Department of Labor statistics on unemployment and poverty . . . or the Equal Employment Opportunity Commission Reports on discrimination in employment.

What all of these make apparent is implicit in the thesis of this book; namely, that we wrestle not with flesh and blood but with principalities and powers. In other words, against systems which freeze men into structural bondage to machines and organizations . . . and against the overweening desire for profits at the expense of persons.

Perhaps the most relevant word asserted here is that the intersection between Malcolm, Martin, Jesse Jackson, Stokely, Don Lee and Vincent Harding is neither Muhammed nor Marx, but Christ, when we understand that in Christ all truth and all authentic things cohere.

Ed Riddick
Director of Research and
Coordinator of Community Issues for
SCLC—Operation Breadbasket

INTRODUCTION

This book is the outgrowth of our experience together. One of us is black and the other white—both Christian. In our communication with each other and with other
people, both black and white, we found the ever present
questions that seem to plague us all: How can Christianity be
updated or redefined to deal with everyday problems of race?
How can the negative images of Christianity be changed? Is
Christ capable of dealing with a black man as a black man?
Should a Christian be concerned about the social needs of
man? Does the Bible really say that whites are superior to
blacks? These and a myriad of other related questions pro-
voked us to examine the facts of history, present social phenomena and the Bible.

We have found that there are more answers available to us
from an objective analysis of the facts than is commonly
believed. We do not pretend to present simple solutions and
answers to all possible questions. But we do believe that the
facts themselves provide us with a basis to deal with personal

and social problems relative to race relations. We do not intend, of course, to offend those who hold attitudes and positions contrary to our own. But having confronted each other with our ignorances and biases, we do feel that our experiences point to the value of human beings thrashing out their differences with one another for the sake of truth.

We believe that Christ is the ultimate solution to the need of men to have harmony with themselves and other men. But some specific solutions are to be found in a deliberate, forceful application of man's knowledge of his past and present. We have found, for example, that many Christians (especially white Christians) tend to ignore or discredit observations and arguments of so-called non-Christians about the racist nature of Christianity. There is much truth in Stokely Carmichael's statement.

> Christians should start working on destroying the church and building more Christ-like communities. It's obvious—that the church doesn't want Christ-like communities. Christ—He taught some revolutionary stuff, right? And the church is a counter revolutionary force.[1]

Mr. Carmichael's opinion is shared by many Americans both white and black. Yet it is especially blacks who have come to view and to experience Christianity as a force which oppresses rather than liberates, as an institution long and fruitfully married to other institutions which have exploited and dehumanized blacks.

It is our opinion that Christianity if viewed objectively, apart from its white racist expression, is indeed a true "revolutionary force." It meets the individual needs of blacks (and whites) who must ultimately relate to the true God who has made himself known . . . Jesus Christ. Thus in the following pages we intend to go beyond the question of racism to the

---

[1] Quoted in Bernard Weinraub, "The Brilliancy of Black," *Esquire*, January, 1968, pp. 48ff.

question of the black man's responsibility to view Christianity independently of white racist definitions and institutional expressions. The purposes of this book are (1) to explain how Christianity relates to the historical and present-day forces which oppress blacks, (2) to show the rejection by blacks of a Christianity which identified itself in such ways, (3) to indicate to blacks the true nature of Christianity and a proper response to this truth and (4) to indicate to white Christians some positive responses to the blacks' demand for a Christianity that meets the objective and subjective needs of the black community.

The reader should understand that we use the term "Christianity" from the perspective of the black oppressed who have come to view it (apart from its denominational differences, *e.g.*, Catholic, Baptist, Methodist) as a monolithic whole. As we will show, the enslavement of blacks was justified in the name of Christianity. Blacks were made to feel cursed in the name of Christianity. Blacks were excluded from white churches in the name of Christianity. Blacks were (and are) excluded from the benefits of American life in the name of a Christianity which blesses the status quo.

Hence, we would like to make it clear that from this point on when we use Christianity in quotation marks we are using it in this broad, popular sense. Because we distinguish between white racist "Christianity" (the broad, popular sense) and true Christianity (used without quotation marks), the reader should be aware of the widest possible difference between these two (see chapter six). It is precisely this distinction that makes it incumbent upon black men to look again at Christianity. They should come to recognize that genuine Christianity affirms a positive black self-concept and actively cooperates with blacks as they struggle to liberate themselves from white oppression.

We would like to acknowledge our appreciation to Rose Torrence who spent many hours typing our original scribble into manuscript form. D. S. and Jim Moore gave invaluable comments and criticisms and we wish to thank them. A special thanks goes to Ed Riddick who during a busy schedule with *Operation Breadbasket* took time to read our manuscript and then write a foreword for it. Finally, Dr. John Warwick Montgomery, Professor of Church History at Trinity Evangelical Divinity School, deserves acknowledgement for providing inspiration and criticism for many of the ideas contained in this work when they were written in another form.

Columbus Salley
English Editor
Harcourt Brace Jovanovich, Inc.
New York

Ronald Behm
Pastor
South Shore Bible Church
Chicago

CHRISTIANITY AND SLAVERY

To develop an appreciation for present-day black attitudes and roles in respect to organized Christianity, we must gain a historical perspective on slavery in the western world. Obviously, slavery had an economic and social dimension. But even more important for our consideration is its psychological impact not only on the slaves but on their posterity. It is this psychological dimension which forms a basis for the present racial conflict in America.

Slavery was an international phenomenon which developed in the United States as one aspect of the expansion of Western European culture into the New World. At one time or another almost every major European power promoted slave trade to North and South America. The Atlantic slave trade was "officially declared open" in 1441 when "ten Africans from the northern Guinea Coast were shipped to Portugal as a gift to Prince Henry the Navigator."[1] Following the dis-

---

[1] John Pope-Hennessy, *Sins of the Fathers: A Study of the Atlantic Slave Traders, 1441-1807* (New York: Alfred A. Knopf, 1968), p. 8.

covery of the New World and for the next three and a half centuries, "and at an ever increasing momentum, the development of the new territories across the Atlantic demanded millions upon millions of African slaves."[2]

While it is difficult to determine how many Africans were captured for the slave trade, estimates range from ten to twenty million.[3] However, "it is more difficult to measure the effect of such an activity on African life" when it is remembered that "traders would have none but the best available slaves" and "that the vast majority of the slaving was carried on in the area of West Africa," the most highly civilized section of the continent with the possible exceptions of Egypt and Ethiopia.[4] Not only was African civilization dealt a severe debilitating blow, but the African slaves themselves who were captured, bought and transported to the New World suffered grossly inhumane treatment at the hands of white captors.

The process of slave "dehumanization" from moment of capture to moment of purchase parallels the concentration camp experiences of World War II. The series of traumatic shocks involved had such an effect upon the Africans that their personality development was altered to suit the image and likeness of a system that assumed their inferiority.

First, there was the shock of being captured. "The second shock—the long march to the sea—drew out the nightmare for

---

[2] *Ibid.*, p. 12.

[3] Frank Tannenbaum, *Slave & Citizen* (New York: Random House, 1946), p. 32. Tannenbaum also notes that many Africans lost their lives and never reached the New World. Of the total some have said "one-third of the Negroes taken from their homes died on the way to the coast and at embarkation stations, and that another one-third died crossing the ocean and in seasoning, so that only one-third finally survived to become the laborers and colonizers of the New World" (pp. 28ff.).

[4] John Hope Franklin, *From Slavery to Freedom: A History of Negro Americans,* 3d ed. (New York: Alfred A. Knopf, 1967), p. 59.

many weeks. . . . Hardship, thirst, brutalities, and near starvation penetrated the experience of each exhausted man and woman who reached the coast."[5] It was also shocking to be sold to foreign traders, and then branded and herded into a strange ship. Then came the protracted and stupefying Middle Passage from Africa to the Americas. This dread transportation involved severe overcrowding, frequent rape, fatal disease and cruel beatings, all of which served to establish a master's absolute domination.[6] The final shock came with a seasoning period in the West Indies during which slaves were taught obedience and cringing submission to their masters.[7]

Black people were first forcibly introduced to the American mainland in 1619 when "Twenty Negars"[8] were sold as indentured servants by a Dutch trader to some inhabitants of Jamestown, Virginia. In this struggling colony, as in the others, there was not a pre-established system of slavery into which the black man could fit. Rather, the slave system and its rationale were forged by whites from latent racist tendencies and from the exigencies of life in the New World. Since white indentured servants or Indian slaves could not provide the permanent labor force for the development of the colo-

[5] Stanley M. Elkins, *Slavery: A Problem in American Institutional and Intellectual Life* (New York: Grosset and Dunlap, 1959), p. 99.
[6] Pope-Hennessy, pp. 97-116, describes briefly the conditions of the Middle Passage.
[7] Elkins (see n. 5 above) outlines this "shock theory" and compares it to the concentration camps of World War II, thus generating considerable debate. Elkins also compares British-American slavery with the slavery of Latin America following Frank Tannenbaum (see n. 3 above) and contends that the Latin system possessed "a fluidity that permitted a transition from slavery to freedom that was smooth, organic, and continuing" (p. 79). Cf. David. B. Davis, *The Problem of Slavery in Western Culture* (Ithaca: Cornell University Press, 1966), pp. 223-61, and Sidney Mintz, Review of *Slavery: A Problem in American Institutional and Intellectual Life* by Stanley Elkins, in *American Anthropologist*, LXIII (June 1961), pp. 579-87.
[8] Winthrop D. Jordan, *White Over Black: American Attitudes Toward the Negro, 1550-1812* (Chapel Hill: University of North Carolina Press, 1968), p. 73. This is a most thorough, careful, scholarly work.

nies, the black man solved the problems.

As an African came to America he was easily "fitted" for his work because he was divorced from his native culture and language. His number was inexhaustible, and his physical characteristics made identification unmistakable. As rationale and justification for the system, he was reputed (falsely) to come from an uncivilized world, thus making slavery the means to the graces of white, Western, "Christian" civilization. W. E. B. DuBois states:

> A system at first conscious and then unconscious of lying about history and distorting it to the disadvantage of the Negroids became so widespread that the history of Africa ceased to be taught. . . . Without the winking of an eye, printing, gunpowder, the smelting of iron, the beginnings of social organization, not to mention political life and democracy, were attributed exclusively to the white race and to Nordic Europe.[9]

Thus, "by the end of the seventeenth century in all the colonies of the English empire, there was *chattel racial slavery* of a kind which would seem familiar to men living in the nineteenth century."[10]

Christianity was a major barrier to be hurdled on the way to chattel racial slavery. There was an unwritten law that a Christian could not be held as a slave.[11] Therefore, if blacks were allowed to be converted, they could no longer be slaves, and baptism would be tantamount to emancipation. This question was not settled in English law until 1729 when "the Attorney-General and Solicitor-General gave their formal opinions that baptism could not alter the temporal condition

---

[9] W. E. Burghardt DuBois, *The World and Africa: An Inquiry into the Part Which Africa Has Played in World History* (New York: International Publishers, 1946), p. 20.

[10] Jordon, p. 98.

[11] Carter G. Woodson, *The History of the Negro Church,* 2d ed. (Washington: Associated Publishers, 1921), p. 2.

of a slave within the British kingdoms."[12]

The colonies themselves did not hesitate to settle the problem much earlier. "If there were any laws, originally enacted to make Christianity more appealing, which might be construed as prejudicial to slavery, this danger could easily be removed by legislative authority."[13] To settle any doubt, the leading colony of Virginia in "a series of laws between 1667 and 1671 laid down the rule that conversion alone did not lead to a release from servitude."[14] Finally the Church of England accepted the position stated by Morgan Godwyn in 1680 that Christianity and slavery were *fully compatible*.[15] Godwyn further argued that Christian faith made slaves better workers and served as security against infidelity and rebellion. The same themes were repeated in the nineteenth century.

With the problem of the status of Christian slaves settled, efforts were made to spread Christianity among the blacks. In 1701 the Society for the Propagation of the Gospel in Foreign Parts (S.P.G.) was organized as a missionary arm of the Anglican Church. Its missionaries who worked among the slaves were opposed by slave masters who were reluctant to allow time to their slaves for religious instruction.

Some difficulty resulted too from the differences of opinion as to what tenets of religion should be taught the Negro and how they should be presented. Should the Negro first be instructed in the rudiments of education and then taught the doctrines of the church or should the missionaries start with the Negro intellect as he [sic] found it on his arrival from Africa and undertake to inculcate doctrines which only the European

---

[12] Davis, p. 209.
[13] *Ibid.*, p. 205.
[14] Oscar Handlin, *Race and Nationality in American Life,* Anchor Books (Garden City: Doubleday and Company, 1957), p. 14.
[15] Davis, pp. 204-05.

mind could comprehend? There was, of course in the interest of those devoted to exploitation, a tendency to make the religious instruction of the Negro as nearly nominal as possible only to remove the stigma attached to those who neglected the religious instruction of their servants.[16]

The Anglican effort had little impact on the slave community. Normally only those slaves closest to the master's family ("house niggers") became converts to Christianity and the greater number of field hands ("field niggers") were neglected.[17]

Those who were influenced were taught doctrine designed to support slavery, almost to the exclusion of the historic dogmas of the Christian faith. So very early in colonial life an intimate and inseparable union between "Christianity" and the institution of slavery was effected. Other religious communions did not engage in significant evangelism or instruction among the blacks until the mid-eighteenth century. In fact, so ineffective was the work that an observer at the close of the American Revolution wrote:

One thing is very certain, that Negroes of that country, a few only excepted, are to this day as great strangers to Christianity . . . as they were at their first arrival from Africa.[18]

Not only were American "Christians" slow and ineffective in presenting the Gospel to their black slaves, but as indicated above they were also guilty of deliberately using the Christian faith to foster docility and obedience.

Through religious instruction the bondsmen learned that

---

[16]Woodson, pp. 19-20.

[17]Joseph R. Washington, Jr., *Black Religion: The Negro and Christianity in the United States* (Boston: Beacon Press, 1964), p. 181. This work, in addition to summarizing historical data, provides a theological analysis of Christianity and black Americans.

[18]William Warren Sweet, *The Story of Religion in America,* rev. and enlarged ed. (New York: Harper and Brothers, 1950), p. 168.

slavery had *divine sanction*, that insolence was as much an offense against God as against the temporal master. They received the Biblical command that servants should obey their masters, and they heard of the punishments awaiting the disobedient slave in the hereafter. They heard, too, that eternal salvation would be their reward for faithful service. . . .[19]

Many slaveholders reported that this kind of religious instruction had favorable effects upon their slaves: There was greater enthusiasm for obedience and less thievery and mischief.[20] At all times, however, the religious activity of the slaves was necessarily supervised by the overseer or the master. Frequently the blacks attended the same churches as the whites to insure proper instruction.[21] Discipline in these white controlled churches was another tool of teaching obedience to the masters. Any infraction of the masters' will was cause for discipline or exclusion from fellowship until genuine repentance was made.[22]

At no time in black slave history did slaves willingly or completely submit to the control of their masters. Because of this fact, a definite and detailed system of subjugation was devised. It might be called

---

[19] Kenneth M. Stampp, *The Peculiar Institution: Slavery in the Ante-Bellum South* (New York: Random House, 1956), p. 158, italics ours.

[20] *Ibid.*

[21] That this "proper instruction" was consistent and effective is witnessed by these words of a North Carolina bondsman recorded in the 1840's and quoted in Gilbert Osofsky, ed., *The Burden of Race: A Documentary History of Negro-White Relations in America* (New York: Harper and Row, 1966), p. 35: "On Sabbath there was one sermon preached expressly for the colored people. I became quite familiar with the texts. 'Servants be obedient to your masters.' 'Not with eye service as man pleasers.' 'He that knoweth his master's will and doeth it not, shall be beaten with many stripes,' and others of this class. . . . The first commandment impressed upon our minds was to obey our masters, and the second was . . . to do as much work when they or the overseers were not watching us as when they were." Osofsky's work has a sermon illustrating these principles on pages 39-44.

[22] Stampp, p. 161.

the way to produce the perfect slave: accustom him to rigid discipline, demand from him unconditional submission, impress upon him his innate inferiority, develop in him a paralyzing fear of white men, train him to adopt the master's code of good behavior, and instill in him a sense of complete dependence.[23]

The "perfect slave" was rarely produced. Instead a slave was constantly watched by the overseer, restricted to his cabin after work hours, unable to leave the estate without a pass and unable "to sell anything without a permit."[24] Slave marriages, as all other aspects of slave life, were under the direct supervision of the masters and had no legal significance. Only the master's consent was necessary for a marriage or a divorce to take place.

Marriage among slaves was a farce, but not because of their low station or ignorance of the ways of the nation. It was so because there could be no marriage where the nation moved monolithically and institutionally to keep all slaves exposed to capricious punishment. . . . By law no slave husband could protect his wife from physical or sexual abuse at the hands of a white man. By law no slave mother could protect her child against physical or sexual abuse at the hands of a white man. These were the reasons why marriage among slaves was meaningless. There could be no functioning family.[25]

. . . The institutional structures of the nation [made] it impossible for the family to serve its primary purpose—*the protection of its members*.[26]

It is highly significant to note that any subsequent intellec-

---

[23] *Ibid.*, p. 148.

[24] *Ibid.*, p. 71.

[25] William H. Grier and Price M. Cobbs, *Black Rage* (New York: Bantam Books, 1968), pp. 68-69.

[26] *Ibid.*, p. 71, italics ours.

tual or psychological response of black people to the institution of slavery would by definition be a response to a "Christianity" which was inextricably united with the oppressive forces of white dominance. Early in the black man's experience with Christianity the image developed in his intrapsychic structure that Christianity is synonymous with whiteness which is synonymous with oppression.

Christianity clarified its image during slavery by using the Bible to defend slavery. J. Oliver Buswell, III, has divided into four groups the historic scriptural justifications for slavery alleged by proslavery clerics and laymen:

(a) general assertions that the institution was natural, "ordained of God," and of benefit to the enslaved; (b) examples of slavery described or alluded to in the Bible, chiefly in the Old Testament; (c) instructions regarding behavior of slaves and masters, chiefly in the New Testament; and (d) underlying the whole structure of the defense system . . . the supposed teachings regarding the Negro race, chiefly based upon elaborations on the story of Ham and the curse of Noah.[27]

Defenders of slavery used these four categories of arguments in various combinations throughout the entire period. As the pressure of criticism coming from various quarters mounted, the biblical defense was maintained with great vigor.[28]

Southern divines gave great diligence to finding biblical support for slavery. They argued that "what God sanctioned in the Old Testament and permitted in the New, cannot be sin."[29] To call slavery a sin against God was therefore to question the authority of God's Word and be guilty of "doc-

---

[27] J. Oliver Buswell, III, *Slavery, Segregation and Scripture* (Grand Rapids: William B. Eerdmans, 1964), p. 12. This work demonstrates that the same four categories of arguments are being used today to defend segregation.

[28] Ralph L. Moellering, *Christian Conscience and Negro Emancipation* (Philadelphia: Fortress Press, 1965), p. 50.

[29] *Ibid.*

trinal heresy." Other defenders of slavery asserted that God's rule of self-preservation and his desire for the good of the slaves required slaveholders to maintain the institution. The Patriarchal system of slavery was designed so that masters should be "a guardian and a father" for their slaves; "freedom would be their doom; and equally from both they call upon us, their providential guardians, to be protected."[30] Noah's curse upon his grandson Canaan to be "a slave of slaves" was applied to all Africans and was supported by fantastic exegesis and erroneous logic.[31]

A Christian minority did make efforts to attack the institution of slavery. In 1688 at the Monthly Meeting near Philadelphia, the Quakers presented a group resolution against slavery. Though the Yearly Meeting did not adopt it, "the resolution expressed a position which would gradually attract more and more Quakers."[32] Antislavery tracts and treatises appeared and an open drive against Quaker slaveholding began. "This crusade, led by Benjamin Lay, John Woolman, and Anthony Benezet, resulted in positive action by the Philadelphia Yearly Meeting in 1758 against both slavetrading and slaveholding by Quakers."[33] Through these efforts many southern Quakers left the South and migrated into the Northwest Territory to avoid collusion with the sin of slavery.[34] By 1800 American Quakers had virtually ceased to be slaveholders.[35] Methodists also have a record of antislavery action. In 1780 the Baltimore Conference required its travel-

---

[30] Osofsky, p. 93.

[31] Buswell, pp. 16-18. See also Charles E. Silberman, *Crisis in Black and White* (New York: Random House, 1964), pp. 172-74. Our rebuttal to this spurious argumentation is included in a later chapter.

[32] H. Shelton Smith, Robert T. Handy, and Lefferts A. Loetscher, *American Christianity: An Historical Interpretation with Representative Documents* (New York: Charles Scribner's Sons, 1963), I, 180.

[33] *Ibid.*

[34] William Warren Sweet, *Religion in the Development of American Culture: 1765-1840* (New York: Charles Scribner's Sons, 1952), p. 279.

[35] Smith *et al.*, p. 293.

ing preachers to set free the slaves which some of them held. They also proclaimed that "slave-keeping is contrary to the laws of God, man and nature, and hurtful to society, contrary to the dictates of conscience and pure religion. . . ."[36]

Christian criticism of slavery diminished after the Revolutionary War, in part at least because the temper of the country stressed unity and peace. Yet when the Abolitionist Movement later flourished, Christian voices were within its ranks. If the Bible could be used for proslavery arguments, it would surely be employed for antislavery arguments. Theodore Dwight Weld, who was a convert of Charles G. Finney,[37] argued that the essential spirit of the Bible opposed all slavery. In his popular and widely distributed work he charged that

ENSLAVING MEN IS REDUCING THEM TO ARTICLES OF PROPERTY—making free agents, chattels—converting *persons* into *things*—sinking immortality into *merchandise.*

We repeat it, THE REDUCTION OF PERSONS TO THINGS! Not robbing a man of privileges, but of *himself*; not loading him with burdens, but making him a *beast of burden*; not restraining liberty, but his neighbour of a *cent*, yet commission him to rob his neighbour of himself? . . . Slaveholding is the highest possible violation of the eight[h] commandment.[38]

Albert Barnes was another leading antagonist of slavery who battled on biblical grounds against "the vicious institu-

[36] *Ibid.,* p. 465.

[37] Gilbert Hobbs Barnes, *The Antislavery Impulse: 1830-1844* (New York: Harcourt, Brace and World, 1964), p. 12. This work caused debate upon its first issue in 1933 by demonstrating that revivalism, especially in the North and the West, contributed greatly to the Abolitionist Movement. Concerning Finney, though he was not an abolitionist agitator, he nevertheless strongly opposed slavery. Cf. Walter Unger, *The Social Views of Charles Grandison Finney,* unpublished M.A. thesis, Trinity Evangelical Divinity School, 1969.

[38] Osofsky, pp. 87-88.

tion."[39]   He met the proslavery argument and adduced his own scriptural evidence to show its fallacious reasoning.

The controversy over slavery naturally had divisive effects upon the Christian denominations. The resolutions against slavery which had been passed by the Methodists were both difficult to enforce and actively opposed. As "the southern states themselves, one by one passed legislation prohibiting" the emancipation of slaves, enforcement became impossible.[40]   This situation also was true for the Baptist groups. However, as the radical and aggressive abolition movement grew in the North and the West and as slavery became an economically and psychologically "necessary" institution of the South, the churches divided over the question of slavery.

It is clear that the institution of slavery served the purpose of concretizing racist attitudes of white domination. The collusion of Christianity with this dehumanizing, oppressive institution made it inevitable for blacks who were the victims of that oppression to conclude that "Christianity" was a mere extension of white racist attitudes and must, therefore, be rejected and destroyed.

---

[39] Moellering, p. 70. Barnes's work is *An Inquiry into the Scriptural Views of Slavery* (Philadelphia: Perkins and Purves, 1846).

[40] Sweet, *The Story of Religion,* p. 291.

CHRISTIANITY AND SEGREGATION

Following the Emancipation Proclamation and the Northern victory in the Civil War there was hope that former slaves would be granted the same rights and privileges that were enjoyed by whites. But there were many obstacles to full equality.

First, the doctrine of black inferiority was held widely both in the North and the South. Whites found social equality for blacks practically inconceivable and many believed that because of the black man's (supposed) innate inferiority he would forever remain in the lower ranks of society. Indeed "some of the abolitionists themselves were ambivalent on the question of Negro equality."[1]

In the second place, the resistance of the South was forceful and fast. Slavery had been destroyed but the "Southern mind" found other ways to perpetuate many of its assumed

---

[1] John Hope Franklin, "The Two Worlds of Race: A Historical View" in *The Negro American*, ed. by Talcott Parsons and Kenneth B. Clark (Boston: Beacon Press, 1964), p. 53.

CHRISTIANITY AND SEGREGATION

benefits. Southerners knew if little or nothing were done to provide the blacks with skills and capital necessary to function as free men, the blacks would remain in subjugation. To maintain white dominance the white response to black freedom was manifested in a series of "Black Codes." Although the Black Codes legalized black marriages, permitted blacks to hold and dispose of property, to sue and be sued, their main purpose was to keep the black "as long as possible exactly what he was: a propertiless rural laborer under strict controls, without political rights, and with inferior legal rights."[2]

Finally, the status of the former slaves prohibited their fulfilling the many privileges and responsibilities of free men. As we have seen earlier, the entire system of slavery was deliberately structured to produce a "plantation mentality," giving the slaves a sense of inadequacy, a negative self-concept and dependency on the white world. Therefore many "free" blacks were inescapably held in bondage to their previous dehumanizing experience. Becoming "free" could not make them educated, stable, independent and self-reliant providers for their families.

The period of Reconstruction has afforded the substance for much historical debate.[3] Its history has great moral overtones and involves the deepest emotions of Southerners and Northerners. In recent years the one-sided interpretation

---

[2] Kenneth M. Stampp, *The Era of Reconstruction, 1865-1877* (New York: Random House, 1965), pp. 79-80.

[3] A good introduction to this debate is *Reconstruction in the South,* ed. by Edwin C. Rozwene (Boston: D. C. Heath and Company, 1952) which is one of the books from the excellent *Problems in American Civilization* series. It contains selections which represent the traditional ("Southern") view and the revisionist view. In addition, E. Merton Coulter in *The South During Reconstruction, 1865-1877,* Vol. III of *A History of the South,* ed. by Wendell Holmes Stephenson and E. Merton Coulter (Baton Rouge: Louisiana State University Press, 1947), supports the traditionalist interpretation. However, Kenneth M. Stampp, *The Era of Reconstruction* and John Hope Franklin, *Reconstruction After the Civil War, The Chicago History of American Civilization,* ed. by Daniel J. Boorstin

which portrayed the Southern whites as victims of a brutal, foolish vengeance has been challenged and properly corrected by many historians.

President Andrew Johnson attempted to implement his inadequate plans for reconstruction during the early months of his administration. When Congress met in the winter of 1865 it refused to admit the (so-called) Johnsonian governments from the eleven states that formed the Confederacy.[4] These governments were chiefly composed of former Confederate leaders and had passed the Black Codes during the time of their brief existence. Thus as the Congress began to develop its reconstruction plans, a great conflict ensued with the President and many of the white Southerners. The Radical Republicans who favored "political equality" and special help for the blacks had real success. Through their efforts the Fourteenth and the Fifteenth Amendments to the Constitution were approved, the Freedmen's Bureau was created and supported, and governments of the Southern states temporarily gave the former slaves political equality. However, the Radicals lost one important battle: The program of land reform was defeated. Kenneth Stampp remarks that

> it meant that their [total] program would have only the most limited economic content; that the Negroes' civil and political rights would be in a *precarious state for many years to come*; and that the radical influence in southern politics would probably collapse as soon as federal troops were removed.[5]

In addition the greatest failure of the Radical Reconstruction

---

(Chicago: University of Chicago Press, 1961), seem to have dealt more accurately with the data as they presented their "revisionist" view. For a brief introduction to this problem see Arnold M. Rose, "Distortion in the History of American Race Relations" in *Assuring Freedom to the Free: A Century of Emancipation in the U. S. A.*, ed. Arnold M. Rose (Detroit: Wayne State University Press, 1964), pp. 27-44.

[4] Stampp, *Era of Reconstruction*, p. 110.

[5] *Ibid.*, p. 129, italics ours.

was that some of its vital features were short-lived. The Freedmen's Bureau which provided emergency relief, schools and protection for the former slaves was disbanded in 1869 after its work had scarcely begun.[6]

The white Southerners who desired to perpetuate black subordination were hardly inactive during this period. The well-known Ku Klux Klan was only one of many volunteer organizations which "expected to do by extra or illegal means what had not been allowed by law: to exercise absolute control over the Negro, drive him and his fellows from power and establish, 'White Supremacy!' "[7] Not only were blacks terrorized and murdered, but the few whites who sympathized with them or helped them were also attacked. Through these and other political efforts the Reconstruction period "came to a gradual end as restraints were relaxed and stringent legislation repealed."[8] Eventually the full-blown system of segregation was legalized and the disenfranchisement of blacks proved successful.[9] "The South's demand that the whole problem be left to the disposition of the dominant Southern white people" was accepted.[10]

By the end of Reconstruction the inequities of blacks *vis-à-vis* whites had persisted. Blacks had been reduced to economic and political powerlessness in a society about to enter the fullness of an industrial age. White institutional racism continued to subjugate and exploit blacks. White racism

---

[6] *Ibid.*, pp. 134-35.
[7] Franklin, *From Slavery to Freedom*, p. 327.
[8] *Ibid.*, p. 329.
[9] There is also recent considerable debate as to the origins of segregation. Joel Williamson, ed., *The Origins of Segregation, Problems in American Civilization* (Boston: D. C. Heath and Company, 1968), provides the best compilation and suggestions for further reading. C. Vann Woodward's *The Strange Career of Jim Crow,* 2d ed. (New York: Oxford University Press, 1966), presents the view that segregation in the South is a relatively late phenomenon. In all of these discussions the gradual and varied nature of segregation should be emphasized.
[10] Woodward, p. 6.

switched from its primary manifestation of slavery to segregation.

The latter decades of the nineteenth century and the early years of the twentieth were marked by great white violence against blacks. The law stood helpless and ineffective while thousands of black men and women were brutally murdered and terrorized. Even the North experienced violent antiblack riots: "New York, 1900; Springfield, Ohio, 1904; Greensburg, Indiana, 1906; Springfield, Illinois, 1908."[11] The blacks were "equal" citizens but they did not receive equal protection under the law.

What role did "white Christianity" play in the segregation period? During the Civil War the churches of both North and South vigorously supported the war effort. People not only prayed for victory (believing that God was on their side) but they also actively worked for victory by encouraging enlistment and offering medical and religious aid. Both the Union and Confederate armies encouraged chaplains in their work. "Literature, provisions and comforts"[12] were provided through churches for soldiers engaged in the terrible conflict. In addition the Northern cause was supported by outstanding church leaders who, at their government's request, travelled abroad to explain and justify the Federal policies. However, despite a great rise in charities and missionary funds contributed by church people, "the cause of vital religion and morals undoubtedly suffered as a result of the war."[13]

The continued political and social involvement of Christian churches can be better understood with this background in mind. "The great northern churches, which had given an almost unanimous support to the government during the stress

---

[11]*Report of the National Advisory Commission on Civil Disorders,* Otto Kerner, Chairman (New York: Bantam Books, 1968), p. 215.

[12]Sweet, *The Story of Religion in America,* p. 317. The information for the present section is taken from Sweet's chapter, "The Churches North and South," pp. 312-26.

[13]*Ibid.,* p. 325.

of the war, felt that they . . . had a . . . duty to take a hand in the solution of reconstruction problems."[14] On the other hand the churches of the South came to be more concerned with defensive activity to support "the Southern way of life."

> The independent regional course of development that the South was permitted to pursue following the Civil War fostered a growing sectional self-consciousness that was to manifest itself in the religious as well as in the political and intellectual life of the southern states.[15]

The three major denominations, Baptists, Methodists and Presbyterians, were unable to reunite after the war because bitterness from the separation and growing sectional interest overruled. The white Southern churches developed a religious style and temperament that was nostalgic and defensive, serving only to widen the gap between themselves and the Northern churches.[16]

More central than the schisms was the fact that the white Southern churches continued black subservience in the name of God.

> The [white] Protestant church, a major southern social institution, was among the first groups to segregate after the Civil War and to accept racism as the basis of race relations. Protestantism *helped pave the way* for the capitulation to racism at the turn of the century.[17]

If blacks felt that they could turn to the "Christian Church" for aid and comfort against the forces of racist attitudes and behavior, they were therefore quickly disillusioned. The image of the irrevocable hostility toward blacks by the white

---

[14]*Ibid.*, p. 327.
[15]Winthrop S. Hudson, *Religion in America* (New York: Charles Scribner's Sons, 1965), p. 203.
[16]*Ibid.*, p. 217.
[17]David M. Reimers, *White Protestantism and the Negro* (New York: Oxford University Press, 1965), p. 25, italics ours.

Christian church was perpetuated. Black men found no solace in the white church.

Though some effort at helping the freedmen was made by the white southern churches, hostile sentiment "in the South soon put an end to almost all official activity."[18] Many black men and women "were anxious to separate themselves from the churches of their former masters" in order to express their freedom and to develop independently from white racist domination.[19] As a result the black church in the South grew rapidly.

Baptist and Methodist churches were by far the most popular among former slaves. The independent African Methodist Episcopal Church and the African Methodist Episcopal Zion Church which had been organized by freedmen in the North during the slavery period experienced phenomenal growth.[20] They were formed largely because the white society would not tolerate the presence of blacks as equals in common public worship. Thus the black churches provided the first institution (and probably the only viable institution) which the freedmen could develop independent from direct white control within the church itself.[21]

The black church, from the period of the Civil War until World War I, has been described as "the accommodative church."[22] The preachers in these churches oriented their members to the domination of the white society. As black ministers had played the role of mediator and spokesman before the Civil War, so they continued during this period. In

[18] Hudson, p. 221.
[19] Sweet, *The Story of Religion,* p. 329.
[20] *Ibid.,* pp. 329-30.
[21] Robert T. Handy, "Negro Christianity and American Church Historiography," in *Essays in Divinity,* Vol. V: *Reinterpretation in American Church History,* ed. by Jerald C. Brauer (Chicago: University of Chicago Press, 1968), pp. 95ff.
[22] Leonard Broom and Norval Glenn, *Transformation of the Negro American* (New York: Harper and Row, 1965), p. 9.

terms of race relations, the black churches' main function was to accommodate its members to their subordinate status in the white society.

The freedom of the Negro preacher was circumscribed by the fact that members of his congregation were in debt to whites or dependent upon whites for their jobs, and the very land on which the church stood was often the property of whites. The preacher was usually easily controlled, but if other means failed, he could be threatened with violence.[23]

The black church not only maintained its function of accommodation by direct admonition but also indirectly by its *other-worldly orientation.*

In providing a structured social life in which the Negro could give expression to his deepest feeling and at the same time achieve status and find meaningful existence, the Negro church provided a refuge in a hostile white world. For [those] who worked and suffered in an alien world, religion offered a means of catharsis for their pent-up emotions and frustrations.[24]

Black minds were turned from the oppression and exploitation of this present world to a future world beyond the grave in which the faithful would be recompensed for all suffering and injustice. And whites were glad to allow their black folks a means of release which helped to keep them submissive. However within this "happy" arrangement the black preacher could often win minor concessions and favors from the white community, so long as his requests did not exceed whatever limits the whites had established. Within this context it is clear that the church provided the only leadership for the black community during the period.

---

23 *Ibid.*
24 E. Franklin Frazier, *The Negro Church in America* (New York: Schocken Books, 1963), pp. 44-45.

The brief day of Radical Reconstruction saw black ministers serve in a great variety of governmental positions.[25] The black church also provided social benefits to its community through its mutual aid societies and its efforts to stabilize the family.[26] At best the black church was a mere black extension of white racist ideology wrapped up in black skins. Eventually blacks would come to view the black church as a perpetuator of white control.

The positive significance of the black church is that it gave blacks a survival style in a hostile world. Its weakness lay in its inability to define afresh the relationship of the black men to God and to their world. Instead the black church reinforced a plantation mentality that established "whiteness" as the standard of fellowship with God and laid the basis for black exclusion in worldly matters.

In contrast to white Southern churches, white Northern churches did provide some help to the black freedman. In particular, this took the form of educational training. Since "through much of the South it had been illegal to teach a slave to read," the greatest need was for literacy instruction.[27] During the years immediately following the war hundreds of Northern teachers, both men and women, went to the South to educate the former slaves. The work was hard and difficult; harassment was common and decent housing was difficult to obtain. "The opposition to the missionary-teacher was based on a determination to keep the Negro 'in his place.' "[28] The total value of this movement was negligible even though many schools were established which later became leading black universities. It dissipated as Radical Reconstruction failed.[29]

---

[25] *Ibid.*, pp. 42-44.
[26] *Ibid.*, pp. 31-42.
[27] Hudson, p. 220.
[28] *Ibid.*, p. 222.
[29] Some schools formed were: "Fisk, Atlanta, and Tougaloo Universities, Talladega College, and Hampton Institute" (*Ibid.*, p. 221).

The zeal the white Northern churches showed for the cause of the black man following the Civil War also waned with the advent of secular and social forces that affected Northern Protestants. "Social Darwinism, racism, and overseas expansion, including foreign missionary work, were among these influences."[30] In addition, desire for national unity and social problems centering in the cities diverted the Northern churches from any strong protest against racial injustice. In fact, "they came close to accepting the South's 'solution' to the race problem."[31]

Racial segregation was expanded in the church and in the schools. Education for blacks began to emphasize industrial and manual skills, thus insensibly fitting blacks for a continued subordinate role in society. Protest against inequalities gave way to unflattering stereotypes of blacks and to paternalistic attitudes. Even leaders within the social gospel movement neglected the racial problem and either adopted notions of racial superiority or refused to rebuke those who did.[32] Yet

> if the proponents of the social gospel neglected the race problem, so did the great revivalists of the late nineteenth and early twentieth centuries. Before the Civil War the evangelic tradition was closely associated with

---

[30] Reimers, p. 52.

[31] *Ibid.,* p. 51.

[32] Thomas F. Gossett, *Race: The History of an Idea in America* (Dallas: Southern Methodist University Press, 1963), p. 193ff. Gossett has shown that Josiah Strong was not followed by clergymen in his zeal for the coming victories of the Anglo-Saxons, neither was he criticized for his racist theories. No clergymen of the period, it would appear, ever attacked him for his unfeeling attitude toward the rights of nonwhite races. From those men from whom we might have expected criticism—such Social Gospel figures as Theodore Munger, Washington Gladden, Walter Rauschenbusch, Lyman Abbott, and George T. Herron—it was not forthcoming. . . . Though it is certainly unlikely that the other leaders of the movement shared Strong's ideas on race, one soon notices in their writings a timidity and a general discomfort in the area of racial theory or the rights of racial minorities."

the antislavery movement and social reform. The later
revivalists tended to shy away from reform movements
and to identify themselves with social conservatism.
. . . In the North, Dwight L. Moody, the famed Chicago
evangelist, *did not protest* against the white man's treatment of the American Negro. When Moody held revival
meetings in the South, he did so on a segregated basis.
. . . Years later, when Billy Sunday went South, he
followed Moody's footsteps and held segregated
meetings.[33]

Any society which deliberately singles out a group of people for a particular type of negative treatment based upon an
unchangeable factor (*e.g.,* skin color) is, in effect, telling
those people that they are not fit to participate in the benefits which naturally accrue to those living in that society. The
overwhelming majority of blacks in America during the segregation period were made to feel a profound and inescapable
sense of personal inadequacy and political and economic impotence. The tragedy of the black experience during segregation was that blacks perceived Christianity as the chief support for the forces of racism that shaped these negative intrapsychic attitudes and social deprivations.

---

[33] Reimers, pp. 54-55, italics ours.

3 CHRISTIANITY AND GHETTOIZATION

Tracing the development of black attitudes toward Christianity we observe, beginning with the twentieth century, one of the most significant phenomena in American history: the mass migration of blacks to the cities of the North and West. Lerone Bennett signalized the importance of this influx by claiming that it nationalized the race problem, gave the Negro a base of potential political power in the North and set the stage for our present confrontation.[1] We refer to this period from approximately 1914 to the present as the ghettoization period in Black American history.

With the advent of this black migration a new and more subtle form of institutional racism developed. Black people were deliberately restricted to certain geographic areas and economic roles within the major cities and similarly reduced to political and economic chattel. The white Christian church

---

[1] Lerone Bennett, Jr., *Confrontation: Black and White* (Baltimore: Pelican Books, 1965).

39

was primarily acquiescent, compliant and complacent in the face of this black subjugation.

The reasons for this migration involved both a "push" and a "pull." The push was the agricultural depression of the South. Increased production of quality cotton in the Southwest, increasing mechanization, the ravages of the boll weevil and a series of floods in the summer of 1915 were primary factors.[2] Another push from the South was the continued terrorism against blacks in the early decades of the twentieth century.

On the other hand there was a great pull from the job opportunities of the industrialized North. Jobs in Southern cities were filled first by whites, leaving little or no work for blacks.[3] So there was a natural and inevitable move northward to fill the labor demand created by World War I and by a series of Immigration Exclusion Acts. Similarly World War II and the post-war boom continued this general demand for black workers in the North.

This geographical redistribution and urbanization had tremendous effects upon the posture, not only of the blacks who migrated, but also of the blacks who remained in the South. Custom was broken and openness to change was expressed. "Many Negroes were never exposed to the idea that they could be equal to whites, and they accepted their inferior status as an unchangeable aspect of the nature of things."[4] Since in the North the open external forms of discrimination when expressed were expressed more subtly, blacks throughout the country began to sense that the Southern status quo was not divinely inspired. Therefore "with the increase in the number of Negroes in cities and in regions

---

[2] Silberman, p. 28. Cf. St. Clair Drake and Horace R. Cayton, *Black Metropolis: A Study of Negro Life in a Northern City,* rev. ed. (New York: Harper and Row, 1962), pp. 58-64.

[3] *Ibid.*

[4] Broom and Glenn, p. 164.

where whites openly espoused the ideal of racial equality, it was inevitable that Negro pressure for elimination of racial discrimination would increase."[5]

Pressure did indeed increase. Urbanization in the concentrated ghettos provided the first opportunity for blacks to develop a sense of community which was combined with close physical proximity. Today it is obvious that ghettoization can produce political power with widespread effects on local and national elections.

The Kerner Report offers an excellent summary highlighting the reaction of whites to the urban influx of blacks since 1914.[6] In 1917 in East St. Louis, Illinois, there was a major antiblack riot issuing from a white fear that blacks were endangering white status. The police did little to hinder white attacks against blacks as "streetcars were stopped, and Negroes, without regard to age or sex, were pulled off and stoned, clubbed and kicked, and mob leaders calmly shot and killed Negroes who were lying in blood in the street."[7] Because the Ku Klux Klan was reorganized and flourishing,

> violence took the form of lynchings and riots, and major riots by whites against Negroes took place in 1917 in Chester, Pennsylvania, and Philadelphia; in 1919 in Washington, D.C., Omaha, Charleston, Longview, Texas, Chicago, and Knoxville and in 1921 in Tulsa.[8]

Racial disorders, usually antiblack riots by whites, continued sporadically during World War II. The Detroit Riot of 1943 was the most destructive and bitter. (However, the black Harlem Riot of 1943 was directed against whites and resulted in destruction of property, looting and burning stores.[9])

The black man's role in the armed forces during the two

---

[5] *Ibid.*
[6] *Report of the National Advisory Commission on Civil Disorders,* pp. 217ff.
[7] *Ibid.,* p. 218.
[8] *Ibid.,* p. 219.
[9] *Ibid.,* p. 224.

World Wars is also indicative of white attitudes and policy.[10] During both wars blacks were forced to serve in segregated units, and only after a long struggle were blacks allowed to train as officers for World War I. Friction, antagonism and discrimination were prevalent phenonema both at home and overseas. However, both of the wars had a positive effect upon the needs of black Americans: They raised the questions of the validity of America's democracy and justice for all citizens and they gave blacks experience in other lands, thereby increasing the desire for change.

The changes that occurred during ghettoization encouraged the protest movement that formed during the early years of this century. Though black men have continually protested their enslavement and subjugation,[11] it was only when the conditions of relative freedom prevailed that mass organizations began to grow.

The National Association for the Advancement of Colored People (NAACP) and the Urban League were the first protest organizations. They were distinctly interracial, believing that the rights of black Americans would be won *within* the American democratic system. In the main, they protested legal blocks to political and economic participation by black Americans. The Congress of Racial Equality (CORE) was formed in 1942 and the Southern Christian Leadership Conference (SCLC), which the late Dr. Martin Luther King, Jr., headed, was begun in 1957.[12] (A later chapter will discuss this protest movement in greater detail.)

We have been at pains to emphasize that racist attitudes

---

[10] Franklin, *From Slavery to Freedom,* pp. 452-76 and 573-600.
[11] Cf. Herbert Aptheker, *Negro Slave Revolts in the United States* (New York: International Publishers, 1939) and Joanne Grant, *Black Protest: History, Documents and Analyses, 1619 to the Present* (Greenwich, Conn.: Fawcett Publications, 1968).
[12] A discussion of these organizations and their philosophies is found in Kenneth B. Clark, "The Civil Rights Movement: Momentum and Organization," in *The Negro American.*

manifest themselves in institutional structures or forms. So it was that the newly-migrated blacks felt the impact of a new form of racism: urban racism. In trying to understand this period of continuing white domination it must be understood that it is not easy to isolate overt racist action.

Maintenance of the basic racial controls is now less dependent upon specific discriminatory decisions and acts. Such behavior has become so well institutionalized that the individual generally does not have to exercise a choice to operate in a racist manner. The rules and procedures of the large organizations have already prestructured the choice. The individual only has to conform to the operating norms of the organization, and the institution will do the discriminating for him.[13]

Urban racism cannot *always* be attributed to some legal statute or explicit policy statement or ideology concerning the worth of black Americans. Instead urban racism represents in a term the synthesis of all white normative values and attitudes toward black values and attitudes, and it is concretized in the major economic, political and social institutions that perpetuate a set of differences between blacks and whites while maintaining a system of white domination.

This helps to explain why blacks are more often unemployed than whites, why blacks must pay higher prices for goods and services than whites, why blacks live in poorer housing than whites, why blacks lack quality education, are relatively powerless politically and find it extremely difficult to break out from the cycle of poverty and despair. Harold Baron describes the vicious cycle of poverty among blacks:

The ghetto provides the base for the segregated schools. The inferior education in ghetto schools handicaps the Negro worker in the labor market. Employment discrim-

---

[13] Harold Baron, "The Web of Urban Racism" in *Institutional Racism in America,* ed. by Louis L. Knowles and Kenneth Prewitt (Englewood Cliffs: Prentice-Hall, Inc., 1969), pp. 142-43.

ination causes low wages and frequent unemployment. Low incomes limit the market choices of Negro families in housing. Lack of education, low level occupations, and exclusion from ownership or control of large enterprises inhibit the development of political power. The lack of political power prevents black people from changing basic housing, planning and educational programs. Each sector strengthens the racial subordination in the rest of the urban institutions.[14]

The movement of the black population from a rural to a predominantly urban setting had a tremendous impact both positively and negatively upon the structure of "white Christianity." The role of "Christianity" during this period did not assume the traditional forms of blatant racist expression. "White Christian" racism took on a more subtle and "acceptable" role and responded in a way that no longer involved it in direct segregating, discriminating and exploiting. Christianity during ghettoization had only to submit quietly to the prevailing racist attitudes and practices which had now become an *inseparable part* of urban institutions. It no longer had to provide explicit theological justification for white dominance in economic, political affairs or for segregation of blacks from whites in housing, education and social institutions. Because white "Christians" had participated in and had supported black subordination throughout American history, it was no longer necessary for the white church to openly espouse white domination. For in reality, the institutions themselves produced a set of differences between whites and blacks which guaranteed this domination.

Therefore, the "sins" of "Christianity" during ghettoization are no longer chiefly the sins of *commission* but of *omission*. This conclusion is not meant to deny the positive reaction of some "Christians" to the injustices perpetrated

---

[14]*Ibid.*

against blacks by the larger white society. It is only intended to show that "Christianity" *as an institution* was, by and large, identified and implicated with the forces of urban racism.

After World War I some white denominations began to take "positive" interest in "the race problem." During the twenties the Ku Klux Klan revived, and racism was evident throughout the country as lynchings and rioting became common. Partly in response to these events, the Commission on Interracial Cooperation was formed and acted "to provide a better social climate for American Negroes, especially in the South."[15]

This interracial movement of the twenties and thirties was, however, often paternalistic and narrow in its goals.

> The importance of the interracial movement should not be exaggerated. In certain respects it reversed the decline of interest in the race problem so noticeable in the decades preceding World War I. . . . It did prod the churches to look at the race problem. . . . But the basic approach of Protestantism to a solution to the race problem still consisted of evangelism and Negro education.[16]

Such a superficial attack by white Christians on the symptoms of white racism did not begin to eliminate the causes of racist exploitation. Clearly, while evangelism and education were good moral efforts and served to soothe the conscience of many white Christians, they did not begin to deal with the harsh realities of white institutional racism. This was, after all, the cause of the social maladies and injustices.

In addition to the interracial movement, many major denominations during the thirties and forties passed resolutions condemning lynchings and brutality, and calling for

---

[15] Reimers, p. 87.
[16] *Ibid.*, p. 95.

equal opportunity. But as Frank Loescher wrote in the late forties, "There is little evidence yet that the convictions of the rank-and-file membership of Protestant denominations are greatly influenced by these official actions."[17] In 1968 Kenneth B. Clark, a leading black social psychologist, expressed the same sentiment:

> It's easy to see. Our churches make words; they pass resolutions. But there is no evidence that the churches have found the strength, the courage or the practical know-how to use religious institutions as instruments for bringing about the kind of maturity [that is necessary for justice in race relations] . . . .[18]

A concrete manifestation of white Christian inability and unwillingness to cope with black people and their needs is expressed in their flight from the black in-migration. Gibson Winter described this white exodus in his work, *The Suburban Captivity of the Churches*:

> Negro in-migration [which] increased rapidly during World War I and after 1920 . . . uniformly accelerated the withdrawal of white Protestantism. . . . The retreat from the Negro occurred in a two-phase movement: higher-status congregations withdrew with the first threat of Negro invasion; middle- and lower middle-class congregations moved more slowly; consequently, the secondary withdrawal of Protestantism came about through attrition.[19]

The "Great White Exodus" reinforced the attitudes of many blacks against an insensitive and irrelevant white "Christianity." The exodus also perpetuated a negative self-concept

---

[17] Frank S. Loescher, *The Protestant Church and the Negro* (New York: Association Press, 1948), p. 7.
[18] Mary Harrington Hall, "A Conversation with Kenneth B. Clark," *Psychology Today*, June 1968, p. 20.
[19] Gibson Winter, *The Suburban Captivity of the Churches* (New York: Macmillan, 1962), p. 50.

among many blacks who had for one reason or another embraced Christianity as a means of finding self-esteem, acceptance and adequacy. But above all, this white reaction to the black in-migration clearly told (and tells) blacks that the "Christian" God was a white God and that he was unwilling and incapable of accepting blacks as equals, unless they first whitened their skins and their souls.

The black church, which had given black people a survival style in a hostile white world, responded to urbanization and white withdrawal by developing a new mental outlook concerning its role in American society. Increasing economic diversity of the black community in the city transformed the accommodative black church into the secular church. As large middle-class and mixed-class congregations grew up in the urban center, the preacher was expected to devote more time to community affairs and the advancement of the race.[20] These activities, as always, were within the accepted limitations of the white power structure and, therefore, consisted largely of improvements in housing, education and the like rather than in "social equality and integration with whites."[21]

Even within this change of perspective by black churches, traditional loyalty to the Baptist and Methodist churches prevailed. But the "predominantly other-worldly outlook" and concern for the purely "spiritual" was diminished.[22] A number of the Northern black ministers became influential in politics and in protest. The Reverend Adam Clayton Powell, Jr., pastor of the huge Abyssinian Baptist Church in New York City, is a prime contemporary example of this. In his book, *Marching Blacks*, he calls for a religion with "ethical integrity" and "moral dynamic" which will transform the

---

[20]Broom and Glenn, p. 13.
[21]*Ibid.*
[22]Frazier, p. 51.

"churchianity" of modern day religion.[23] Thus, there had crystallized among the mass of black church people a new concept of the role of Christianity in everyday life situations and of the potential of blacks to function in a more effective way in attacking the social injustices and inequities caused by white institutional racism.

Yet it was to be left to blacks who repudiated "Christianity" as white (and therefore, inhuman and oppressive by its very nature) to create the atmosphere for black people to redefine their whole lives independent of white "Christian" values. Because "Christianity" in the thinking of these awakened blacks had become synonymous with the forces that deprived black people of a positive self-concept and of equal political, economic and social participation in our society, any future effort to "Christianize" blacks would be met with the response *"Your God is too white!"*

Our purpose is not to justify this response but to acknowledge legitimate reasons that black people have for rejecting Christianity based upon white Christianity's perennial racist posture. It is an indisputable fact that white men did use their version of Christianity to defend the peculiar institution and pacify their slaves. White men did relegate their black Christian brothers to separate pews and galleries and, finally, separate churches. White men have oppressed black men and women in the name of the God of the Bible throughout the entire history of America.

Pierre Berton, in *The Comfortable Pew*, issues this charge:
Indeed, the history of the race struggle in the United States has been to a considerable extent the history of the Protestant rapport with the status quo. From the beginning, it was the church that put its blessing on slavery and sanctioned a časte system that continues to

---

[23]Adam Clayton Powell, Jr., *Marching Blacks* (New York: Dial Press, 1945), p. 198-99.

CHRISTIANITY AND GHETTOIZATION

this day. This has prepared the way for the system of class structure within the Protestant church that exists throughout the Western world. It is a negation of that Christian equality before God which the church preaches.[24]

This hypocrisy, Berton maintains, is what has driven away many thousands from the organized Protestant religions. Moreover, those who are "most violently opposed to white supremacy" are also fierce opponents of Christian faith,[25] because "the church has been tried on the most fundamental Christian issue and found wanting."[26]

James Baldwin expressed similar attitudes in an interview when he said that black "people are repudiating the Christian church in toto." His white interviewer probed, "Are they repudiating Christianity as well?" Baldwin shot back, "No more intensely than you have." When further pressed about whether the black church was dead in the North, Baldwin replied, "Let me rephrase it. It does not attract the young. Once that has happened to any organization, its social usefulness is at least debatable."[27]

Thus at present, there is a widespread disillusionment among blacks with Christianity. Black people know they *must* redefine their identity in order to survive with dignity in a racist society, and to this end "Christianity" has proved a menace.

---

[24]Pierre Berton, *The Comfortable Pew* (Philadelphia: J. B. Lippincott Company, 1965), p. 29.
[25]*Ibid.*, p. 31.
[26]*Ibid.*, p. 31.
[27]James Baldwin, "How Can We Get the Black People to Cool It?" *Esquire,* July 1968, pp. 48ff.

4 GLIMPSES OF THE NEW IDENTITY

The historical review of the first three chapters has shown us the experience of black Americans with institutions that sought to destroy or negate any sensitivity of black people to their humanity and culture. During the slavery period the conditions of black people were so structured that a personality type consistent with racist ideology was produced. Black people were ripped from their native culture by a series of atrocities, deprived of a viable family unit, made to feel completely dependent upon white masters and deliberately exposed to white values and standards that reinforced their negative self-concept.

During the segregation period white Americans continued to deny blacks full participation in the economic, political and social spheres of American life. Ghettoization brought with it a new form of institutional racism. An interlocking and self-enclosed network of poor education, substandard housing, unemployment, a paucity of community services and political impotency deprived blacks of the full benefits of American life.

The role of Christianity has been firmly established in relationship to these oppressive institutional forces. Because of the inseparable nature of this relationship, many blacks have been made to feel that Christianity is synonymous with white exploitation, dehumanization of blacks and in general the perpetuation of white domination and black subordination. Christianity is viewed by these blacks as the last major obstacle to their attempt to recapture a sensitivity to their humanity and culture and to redefine their role in a white racist society.

The necessity for black Americans to redefine themselves should be evident to all. Any people who have been deprived of an understanding of their past and of a positive "people-concept" cannot hope to function as an equal and potent power in any society. Black people in America have been deliberately deprived by white institutional forces of a sense of self-worth, thus reducing their majority to a state of psychological disarray and *de facto* powerlessness.

A positive or negative people-concept with its resulting self-concept among its members is not the exclusive product of group or internal psychological phenomena. Voices and images from the external world ultimately affect how the group and the individual view themselves. The white, American, "Christian" society in the periods of slavery, segregation and ghettoization expressed the opinion that those things associated with *black* culture were evil, vulgar, diseased and primitive and that those things associated with the white culture were virtuous, beautiful, Godlike and worthy of emulation by all. Racial dignity demands that black Americans divest themselves of these negative aspersions cast upon them by whites.

In tracing the present day black disillusionment with Christianity, one must understand that throughout the history of this country there were many blacks who rejected what appeared to be the white "Christian concept" of the worth and value of black people. This chapter will consider the response of a few representative blacks who rejected whiteness as the standard of goodness and rejected Christianity as an oppressive tool in the hands of whites who wanted to rob blacks of their full humanity and citizenship. Such an active protest in assertion and pursuit of a positive black identity laid the foundation for all blacks who came after. Today's Black-power, Black-identity movement is the current expression of these historical manifestations.

In the late 1700's Richard Allen and Absalom Jones asserted the positive desire for black participation and equality in those things which were considered "Christian." But being excluded from equal participation in Methodist church life, the two men departed from the traditional relations between black people and white institutions, both secular and religious. The incident which precipitated this change took place in November of 1787 in Philadelphia.

Two prominent Negro leaders—Richard Allen and Absalom Jones—and several of their friends entered the St. George Methodist Episcopal Church for a regular Sunday service. Large numbers of Negroes had been drawn to this church and had been permitted to occupy comfortable seats on the main floor, but the increasing popularity of St. George's finally prompted church officials to announce that henceforth Negroes would be expected to sit in the gallery. Aware of this new seating arrangement, Allen, Jones, and other Negroes took seats in the front of the gallery, overlooking the places which they had previously occupied. But the church authorities had actually reserved an even less conspicuous place for their Negro worshipers in the rear of the gallery, and they soon made this quite apparent. "We had not been long upon our knees," Allen later recalled, "before I heard considerable scuffling and low talking. I raised my head up and saw one of the trustees . . . having hold of the Reverend Absalom Jones, pulling him up off his knees, and saying, 'You must get up—you must not kneel here.' " Jones thereupon requested that the officials wait until the prayers had been completed. When the trustees persisted, however, and threatened forcible removal, "we all went out of the church in a body and they were no more plagued with us." In fact, "we were filled with fresh vigor to get a house to worship God in."[1]

This event led to the formation of two separate black denominations. Absalom Jones organized the African Protestant Episcopal Church of St. Thomas, and Richard Allen (in 1816) became the bishop of the African Methodist Episcopal Church which he founded. Lerone Bennett, commenting upon the importance of this separation of blacks from white racist churches, states:

> By withdrawing from the white Methodist church, the little band of Negro Protestants affirmed the *new image* they had of themselves as human beings who demanded certain minimum concessions to their humanity. . . . The withdrawal raised large questions of identity.[2]
>
> They then embarked on a perilous journey of self-naming, self-legitimization, and self-discovery.[3]

Christianity, as it was then expressed, was unwilling and incapable of providing (1) equal participation for blacks and (2) a set of values and ideals which would allow black people to view themselves positively. Therefore, this action of Richard Allen and Absalom Jones in forming and controlling separate black churches is an early glimpse of the use of

---

[1] Leon F. Litwack, *North of Slavery: The Negro in the Free States, 1790-1860,* Phoenix Books (Chicago: University of Chicago Press, 1961), p. 191.

[2] Bennett, p. 44, italics ours.

[3] *Ibid.,* p. 43.

positive self-image and of power to build an independent base of true *black* expression in America. This too was a rejection by blacks of the "Christian" God who is too white and by virtue of his whiteness is incapable of empowering his followers to accept blacks as equals.

Another significant departure in the thinking of blacks toward their role in white society was revealed in Nat Turner's 1831 slave rebellion. Nat Turner was a self-taught black slave who very early in his life rejected the notion that blacks were inferior to whites. Much of his thinking about his own equality and worth came from the Bible. Naturally therefore he rejected the white "Christian" teaching that blacks were cursed of God and meant to serve whites the rest of their lives. Nat Turner considered himself a divine appointee to execute God's judgment against whites. He states in his *Confessions*:

> ...On the 12th of May 1828, I heard a loud noise in the heavens, and the Spirit instantly appeared to me and said the Serpent was loosened, and Christ had laid down the yoke he had borne for the sins of men, and that I should take it on and fight against the Serpent, for the time was approaching when the first should be last and the last should be first.[4]

Not only was Nat Turner motivated by what he felt was a divine-given mission to destroy whites, but he also seemed to be obsessed with a desire to obtain his own freedom. In August of 1831, Nat Turner and a band of sixty to eighty black compatriots roamed the countryside of South Hampton, Virginia, terrorizing, killing (45 whites) and demonstrating black resistance to slavery.

The significance of this slave rebellion for our purposes here is that a representative number of blacks rejected the

---

[4] Herbert Aptheker, *Nat Turner's Slave Rebellion* (New York: Grove Press, Inc., 1966), p. 43.

traditional white American "biblical" justification for black inferiority and sensed that they could be used as an instrument in the hand of the true God (who obviously accepted their equality and worth) to destroy whites who carried on injustices against blacks. W. E. B. DuBois interpreted Nat Turner's rebellion as a repudiation of the accepted notion that black people are nobodies:

Why strive to be somebody? The odds are overwhelming against you—wealth, tradition, learning and guns. Be reasonable. Accept the dole of charity and the cant of missionaries and sink contentedly to your place as humble servants and helpers of the white world.[5]

Another prominent black protest leader, Frederick Douglass, vented his indignation with white "Christian" hypocrisy that forced blacks to sit in an "African corner," a "Nigger Pew," in seats marked, "B. M." for Black Members, or in the balcony, "Nigger Heaven."

Attending a Methodist service in New Bedford, Frederick Douglass found himself placed in a separate seat and saw his brethren stand meekly aside as the whites attended the Lord's Supper. The pastor then called upon his "colored friends" to come forward, declaring, "You, too, have an interest in the blood of Christ. God is no respecter of persons." By this time Douglass had had enough. "The colored members—poor, slavish souls —went forward as invited. I went *out*, and have never been in that church since."[6]

Frederick Douglass further denounced the "Christian" attitude toward black people in a speech in Rochester, New York, on July 5, 1852. He expressed not only his own feelings, but the emotions of black men of all ages.

But the Church of this country is not indifferent to the

---

[5] Quoted in Herbert Aptheker, *Nat Turner's Slave Rebellion*, p. 107.
[6] Litwack, p. 209.

wrongs of the slaves. It actually takes sides with the oppressors. It has made itself the bulwark of American slavery, and the shield of American slave-hunters. Many of its most Eloquent Divines, who stand as the very lights of the Church, have shamelessly given the sanction of religion and the Bible to the whole slave system. They have taught that man may properly be a slave; that the relation of master and slave is ordained of God; that to send back an escaped bondman to his master is clearly the duty of all the followers of the Lord Jesus Christ; and this horrible blasphemy is palmed off upon the world for Christianity.

For my part, I would say, welcome infidelity! Welcome atheism! Welcome anything! In preference to the gospel, as preached by those Divines! They convert the name of religion into an engine of tyranny and barbarous cruelty. . . . These ministers make religion a cold and flinty-hearted thing, having neither principles of right action nor bowels of compassion. They strip the Love of God of its beauty and leave the throne of religion a huge, horrible, repulsive form. It is a religion for oppressors, tyrants, man stealers, thugs. . . . A religion that favors the rich against the poor: which exalts the proud above the humble; which divides mankind into two classes, tyrants and slaves; which says to the man in chains, *Stay there* and to the oppressor, *Oppress on!!*[7]

Many of the same sentiments were expressed early in the twentieth century by W. E. B. DuBois. DuBois was one of the seminal thinkers of the black protest-identity movement. His opinions of Christianity and its role *vis-à-vis* the black struggle in America against oppressive, dehumanizing forces were succinctly expressed in 1931.

---

[7] Carter G. Woodson, ed., *Negro Orators and Their Orations* (Washington, D. C.: Associated Publications, 1925), p. 215.

The church, as a whole, insists on a divine mission and guidance and the indisputable possession of truth. Is there anything in the record of the church in America in regard to the Negro to prove this? There is not. If the treatment of the Negro by the Christian Church is called "divine," this is an attack on the conception of God more blasphemous than any which the church has always been so ready and eager to punish.[8]

According to DuBois, the validity of Christianity stands or falls with the Christian church's actions. It is understandable that such a man, greatly influenced by his vast historical research concerning the destructive role of Christianity in relation to black people, would conclude that Christianity (as it was then expressed and structured) was totally incapable of helping black people redefine and reorder their existence in American society.

The white concept of God, goodness, beauty and truth was frequently expressed by black writers during the period of ghettoization. With the Harlem Renaissance of black expression in a great variety of literary forms, the theme of "God is white" was often manifested. Langston Hughes, in his popular Jesse B. Semple stories, wrote of the impressions that Semple had of the experience of heaven for a black man. Semple, after being told that he must be born again to erase his birthmark of blackness, retorted by saying,

And washed whiter than snow. . . . Imagine all my relatives setting up in heaven washed whiter than snow. I wonder would I know my grandpa were I to see him in paradise? Grandpa Semple crowned in Glory with white wings, white robe, *white skin* and golden slippers on his feet! Oh, Grandpa, when the chariot swings low to carry me up to the Golden Gate, Grandpa, as I enter will you identify yourself—*just in case I do not know you,* white

---

[8] Quoted in Reimers, p. 180.

and winged in your golden shoes? I might be sort of turned around in heaven, Grandpa.[9]

Jesse B. Semple's representative Negro desire to become white is revealed in his conversation with Saint Peter and a white Southern Governor at the gate of heaven. The Governor insisted that Jesse enter heaven through the back COLORED ENTRANCE, and when Saint Peter could do nothing, Jesse said

I did not realize I was in hell. . . . I thought when I riz through space from my dying bed, I had landed at the Gate of Heaven. Anyway, Peter, is not my sins washed whiter than snow? Am I not *white now inside and out*?'

Whereupon, Old Down-home Governor spoke up and said, 'You have to bathe in the River of Life to be washed whiter than snow. The River of Life is in heaven. You are not inside yet, Semple. Therefore, you are still black. White is right, black get back! You are not coming in the front entrance. [10]

Although Jesse B. Semple is a fabricated character who moves through the hostile world of Harlem, he nevertheless accurately reflects the experiences of many blacks with white Christianity. In particular James Baldwin, in relating his own personal life in Harlem and the need for young blacks to get a "gimmick" in order to survive amid the oppressive and destructive forces created by urban racism (such as sexual perversity, drugs and racketeering), tells of his encounter with the "white God." Baldwin determined that his gimmick for survival in Harlem would be the church. He relates that while in church one summer night he fell victim to the strangest sensations of his life after hearing a woman preach. He began clapping and singing, stomping and falling to the floor trying to get a "salvation experience." At his highest moment

---

[9] Langston Hughes, *Semple's Uncle Sam* (New York: Hill and Wang, 1968), p. 20, italics ours.
[10] *Ibid.*, pp. 95ff, italics ours.

of emotion and ecstacy he looked up from the floor to God as a last resort to give him a sense of power and acceptance. He revealed his innermost feelings and sense of frustration by saying, "But God—and I felt this even then, so long ago, on that tremendous floor, unwillingly—is *white*. . . . I found no answer on the floor—not *that* answer, anyway—and I was on the floor all night."[11]

James Baldwin was a black man seeking an experience with God in a white man's world. He was driven away from God because of his acute awareness of Christianity's identification with oppressive and dehumanizing institutions. Baldwin represents the commonality of experience for many blacks with white Christianity. Like Jesse B. Semple, he is typical.

Every significant movement against human injustices and atrocities goes through a period of expression in which one man eloquently carries the grievances and agonies of the oppressed people. Malcolm X, in our opinion, represents that black man who eloquently and lucidly stated the black man's case against white Christianity. He symbolizes a redefined black man who has now found meaning, worth and value independent of white definitions and values.

Malcolm X demanded of his black brothers that they throw off every vestige of whiteness in order to be free men and find a new source of power consistent with their rediscovered humanity. To Malcolm, high on the list of negative forces and ideologies to be destroyed was Christianity. It must be exposed as inextricably united with oppressive forces in a racist society and it must be rejected as a religion which seeks to rob black people of their humanity and deprive them of the physical means whereby they can correct social injustices.

In his widely-circulated *Autobiography* Malcolm pointedly states:

---

[11] James Baldwin, *The Fire Next Time* (New York: Dell Publishing Co., 1968), p. 46, italics ours.

> Christianity is the white man's religion. The Holy Bible
> in the white man's hands *and his interpretations of it*
> have been the greatest single ideological weapon for en-
> slaving millions of non-white human beings.[12]

Malcolm builds his case for the black rejection of Christianity
by maintaining that black people

> were supposed to be a part of the "Christian Church,"
> yet we lived in a bitter world of dejection . . . being re-
> jected by the white "Christian Church." In large num-
> bers we became victims of drunkenness, drug addiction,
> reefer smoking . . . in a false and futile attempt to
> "escape" the reality and horror of the shameful condi-
> tion that the Slavemaster's Christian religion had placed
> us in.[13]

Malcolm puts the final touches to his denunciation of white
"Christianity" as a destructive force in operation among
black people by citing its greatest failure to eliminate racism
within its own structures. He asks,

> And what is the greatest single reason for this Christian
> church failure? It is the failure to combat racism. It is
> the old 'You sow, you reap' story. The Christian church
> sowed racism—blasphemously; now it reaps racism.

It is of paramount importance to empathize with the experiences of these black protesters and to understand their
subsequent rejection of a hollow, hypocritical and racist
Christianity. Their experiences represent the inner-psycho-
logical responses of countless black people to a white God
who is associated with forces that seek to deliberately make
black people insensitive to their humanity and politically and
economically powerless.

We live in a day in which many black people feel it impera-

---

[12] Malcolm X, *Autobiography* (New York: Grove Press, 1965), p. 241, italics
ours.
[13] C. Eric Lincoln, *The Black Muslims in America* (Boston: Beacon Press, 1961),
pp. 69-70.

tive to redefine themselves independently from all white standards, values and definitions. This phenomenon is understandable because *no people consciously and deliberately move toward that which they believe will destroy their basic humanity*. Therefore, we are seeing a total rejection of white Christianity by many blacks who seek a new identity of pride and *power* both corporate and personal.

5

THE EMERGENCE OF BLACK POWER: THE BASIS FOR A NEW RELIGION

A survey of the black protest against white Christianity reveals widespread black disillusionment and rejection of the basic values, assumptions and attitudes of white, American "Christianity." "Christianity" as the "national religion" has become synonymous with the oppressive institutions of white racism which seek to perpetuate the social, economic and political subordination of black Americans. It has, in effect, done its greatest damage in conditioning black people to hate themselves and all things associated with blackness. People who hate themselves are not psychologically equipped to function as equal and potent members of any society.

Black people sense today (and have always sensed) that black-skinned Americans must redefine themselves and their role *according to their own* values, assumptions and goals in order to survive *as men* in a white racist society. The tragedy of the black experience in relation to "Christianity" is that "Christianity" (as manifested through its association with dehumanizing institutions and their values) was and is unable to provide blacks with the necessary basis to free themselves from white oppression and a sense of inferiority. Thus, there has crystallized within the black community a black consciousness and sensitivity to their own humanity and to their own past and future. This new awareness and its social expression is called *Black Power.*

Black Power in our opinion is both a *subjective* and an *objective* force; subjective in that the black individual's psychological constitution is refocused on his humanity and worth; objective in that black people collectively express a consciousness of this redefined self when they deal with institutions which subordinate them. We will deal with each manifestation in turn.

Subjectively, the negative forces in operation during the periods of slavery, segregation and ghettoization have had the collective effect of creating in the minds of many black people doubts concerning their human worth and dignity. The humanity of blacks in America was primarily left to be determined by the opinions and attitudes of the dominant white society. America's founding fathers assumed it was within their power and responsibility to debate, compromise and negotiate the human worth of black people. Probably no other single issue has created more conflict and division among whites in this country. The power of white "Christian" society to define the ultimate worth of black people and of the value of blackness has created within the psyche of blacks a doubt about their human equality with whites. W. E. B. DuBois expressed the black man's uncertainty by posing the following queries:

> To be sure behind the thought lurks the afterthought: suppose if all the world is right and we are less than men? Suppose this mad impulse is all wrong, some mock mirage from the untrue? . . . a shriek in the night for the freedom of men who themselves are not yet sure of

their right to demand it?[1]

Black Power is the bold assertion of the fact that the humanity of blacks is a non-negotiable, indisputable, non-compromising reality. The humanity of black people *is*!

Black Power is *initially* the psychological realization that white oppressive, dehumanizing institutions are only capable of making blacks insensitive to their humanity; that no man or institutional form has the power to destroy the basic humanity of black people. The reality of the humanity of blacks is independent of racist attitudes and values. The humanity of blacks is as certain as the forces used by God to regulate the universe, as real as the principles that dominate life and death.

A people and the institutions that reflect their values are inhuman and oppressive when they deliberately single out another people for the purpose of subjugation and make them more concerned with survival in a hostile environment than with basic human issues—Who am I? Where did I come from? Where am I going? What is to be my role and the role of others like me in the larger society?

Regardless of the extensive economic, political and educational control whites have held over blacks, the essential white power in America must ultimately be measured by white ability to control the black minds. For any people that can dictate the terms and definitions by which another people define themselves possesses real power. Black Power acknowledges that.

Thus any black revolution against forces of destruction and exploitation *must* begin at the level of the mind. Black Power begins with the realization that blacks have been conditioned by white institutions to hate themselves and to question their basic worth. After a confrontation with these nega-

---

[1] W. E. Burghardt DuBois, *The Souls of Black Folk* (New York: Fawcett World Library, 1961), p. 75.

tive psychic forces, Black Power reaffirms the indestructibility of black humanity and actively seeks values and definitions that will allow blacks to redefine and reorder their lives in white America.

The normative values of our "Christian" culture make it impossible for blacks to view themselves as equals with whites. The very institutions that reflect white America's values are predicated on the assumption and ideal of the superiority of whites and the inferiority of blacks. These values have already been shown to exist in white Christian society's justification of the enslavement of blacks and in its justification of their continued economic and political powerlessness.

Black Power as a force drives the "newly sensitized black man" back to Africa to find his existence and a sense of history independent of the Sambo plantation-induced mentality. He is made to see that the glory of the ancient kingdoms of Ghana, Mali, Songhay and so forth—the splendor and the power, the agonies and the joys, the contributions of Ethiopia and Egypt—are his. Africa *functions* to make black men see that they had a culture and a history *independent* of white racist America. Though his humanity cannot in reality be defined by anyone, the questions that lurk in his bosom about his human worth and value have now been resolved: "I am human—proud, indomitable, irrepressible!"

An awareness of the black contribution to American life also gives "the redefined black" greater certainty of his human qualities and worth. He sees, amid the negative and destructive forces created by white racism, that black men and women such as Benjamin Banneker, Harriet Tubman, Denmark Vesey, Gabriel Prosser and Marcus Garvey (most of whom whites have never heard of!) not only helped develop a survival style and culture uniquely black, but also made contributions of lasting value to the larger American society.

Black Power is a repudiation of the notion that the black

experience in America is maladaptive, pathological and diseased. Rather, it is a demonstration of the desire and power of a people to survive and excel.[2]

This subjective concept of Black Power is not shared by all "black-skinned" Americans. It is vital that distinctions be made between types of black-skinned people on the basis of their demonstrated sensitivity (or insensitivity) to Black Power as a subjective force. We believe there are three broad types of black-skinned people in America: black, Negro and "nasty nigger."

A *black man* is an individual who has had a home-coming to his blackness, who has repudiated white concepts and values about his role and worth in America. He defines himself using his own terms, definitions and values. The black man believes that one must use whatever means necessary to deal with oppressive forces created and perpetuated by white racism.

The *Negro* is a black-skinned person with a white mind. He has set his whole life in motion toward emulating and approximating the white world; he wants to look white, think white and behave white. Because of his controlled participation in the pursuit of materialism, the Negro is made to believe that all is not as bad as stated by blacks and other dissidents.

The *"nasty-nigger"* is the personification of all those negative and distorted white concepts of the nature and worth of blacks. He usually represents the epitome of the white concepts of black sexual prowess, recklessness, proclivity toward crime, etc. He is the modern day result of the negative conditioning of white institutional racism. He hates himself and other blacks. The "nasty nigger" is insensitive to his humani-

---

[2] Grier and Cobbs, in *Black Rage,* pp. 50-62, analyze the survival style of black Americans as expressed through the lives of black women. Their conclusion is that any style of life which perpetuated human life under such dehumanizing conditions has to be an expression of good, normal human adjustment.

ty and daily falls victim to the direct exploitation and oppression of white society.

We realize that definitions and categories of the type which we have given cannot possibly describe all the responses of black-skinned people to oppression and discrimination.[3] But it is our belief that the above analysis reveals their basic, characteristic response to racist forces.

The failure to recognize these differences can have catastrophic results for those who are trying to understand and cope with the black inner-psychic revolution. Many, for example, may feel that by dealing with the Negro they are helping to solve the racial problem in America; they are not cognizant of the fact that the Negro's basic viewpoint on life makes him just as oppressive and threatening to blacks as the white world is. Therefore, it is imperative that one sincerely concerned with being a part of the solution to the problems of racism recognize and have appropriate dealings with all three types of black men.[4]

The concept of Black Power as a *subjective force* among blacks is summarized by Carmichael and Hamilton as

the need [of blacks] to assert their own definitions, to

---

[3] Brewton Berry in *Race and Ethnic Relations*, 2d ed. (Boston: Houghton Mifflin Company, 1958), p. 475ff., lists four different sets of patterns of adjustment to discrimination. His own consists of (1) acceptance, (2) avoidance, (3) assimilation and (4) aggression. The unique and revealing method employed by S. M. Strong in "Negro-white Relations as Reflected in Social Types," *The American Journal of Sociology,* LII (July 1946), pp. 23-30, and recorded in Berry, pp. 468-69, uses the language employed by blacks at that time: (1) the "white man's nigger" ("Uncle Tom"), (2) the "bad nigger," (3) the "smart nigger," (4) the "white man's strumpet," (5) the "mammy," (6) the "sheet lover," (7) the "race leader," (8) the "race man," (9) the "race woman." Thomas F. Pettigrew's *A Profile of the Negro American* (Princeton: D. Van Nostrand Company, Inc., 1964) and Abram Kardiner's and Lionel Ovesey's *The Mark of Oppression: Explorations in the Personality of the American Negro* (Cleveland: World Publishing Co., 1951) should also be seen for more information on this point.

[4] It is very likely that any one black-skinned American can exhibit characteristics of all three psychological types—black, Negro or "nasty nigger"—in response to the white world. Nor should these categories be understood as being fixed and

reclaim their history, their culture; to create their own sense of community and togetherness. There is a growing resentment of the word "Negro," for example, because this term is the invention of our oppressor; it is *his* image of us that he describes. Many blacks are now calling themselves African-Americans, Afro-Americans or black people because that is *our* image, stereotypes—that is, lies—that our oppressor has developed will begin in the white community and end there. The black community will have a positive image of itself that *it* has created. This means we will no longer call ourselves lazy, apathetic, dumb, good-timers, shiftless, etc. Those are words used by white America to define us. If we accept these adjectives, as some of us have in the past, then we see ourselves only in a negative way, precisely the way white America wants us to see ourselves. Our incentive is broken and our will to fight is surrendered. From now on we shall view ourselves as African-Americans and as black people who are in fact energetic, determined, intelligent, beautiful and peace-loving.[5]

As we have defined Black Power, the subjective (psychological) force must manifest itself in objective reality. The initial psychological forces as analyzed *are not enough in themselves to emancipate an oppressed people.*

A people are not simply "free" when they have unshackled their minds from the negative concepts and values of the oppressor; they are "free" when the combined forces of the mind and the body unite with others of the same experience

---

unchangeable. Thus many Negroes and "nasty niggers" are in "transition" toward that which is black.

The viability and potentiality of the Black Power movement is directly proportional to the ability of blacks to establish a working rapport with "nasty niggers." This working rapport maintains the pressure on white society (and Negroes) to recognize the legitimacy of the black protest.

[5] Stokely Carmichael and Charles V. Hamilton, *Black Power: The Politics of Liberation in America* (New York: Vintage Books, 1967), pp. 37-38.

to deal with the institutions which keep them in economic and political slavery.

The Grand Inquisitor, in Dostoyevsky's great work, *The Brothers Karamazov,* observed that the real ruler of men is "he who holds their conscience *and their bread* in his hands."[6] Black Power wisely recognizes that black people will always be victimized and dominated by white society if blacks do not control their economic and political destiny. Aimé Cesaire, in his speech at the Conference of Negro-African Writers and Artists in 1956 as reported by James Baldwin, expressed this truth:

> All cultures have . . . an economic, social, and political base, and *no culture can continue to live if its political destiny is not in its own hands.* "Any political and social regime which destroys the self-determination of a people also destroys the creative power of that people."[7]

Thus if the black community is to manifest its values and ideals in ways which affirm and express its full humanity, it must deliberately structure its daily affairs and institutions. Black people must establish independent and viable bases of economic and political power. To many Americans such an independent base of Black Power would seem to be synonymous with separatism and black racism. However, in a pluralistic society like our own in which blacks are victims of white domination, it is an absolute necessity for black people to develop independent power bases if they are to assure themselves and their posterity of the legacy of the black experience and of equal opportunities free from white racist control.

No people can in reality be said to possess power as long as they continue to simply *react* to oppressive forces. The objec-

---

[6] Fyodor Dostoyevsky, *The Brothers Karamazov,* trans. by Constance Garnett (New York: The New American Library, 1957), p. 238, italics ours.

[7] James Baldwin, *Nobody Knows My Name* (New York: Dell Publishing Co., 1963), p. 38, italics ours.

tive power of a people can be measured by their ability to initiate and control their own circumstances. This reality means that black people must control the *educational systems* that teach their young. Only in this way can black children learn to develop a positive self-concept and a desire for political, economic and social participation both within and without the black community. They must *see* black men and women in decision- and policy-making positions in their educational system in order to encourage and reinforce a sense of adequacy and competence.

This reality means that black people must control their *political representatives* so that the needs and desires of their community are consistently expressed and met at all levels of government. Any political coalitions will be to the mutual benefit of the black community and all others involved. This reality means that black people must support black enterprises so as to establish an economic base initially among blacks that will ultimately allow black entrepreneurs to participate in the larger American economy in viable coalitions.

This understanding of Black Power in its objective expression in the educational, political and economic spheres finds a classic statement by Stokely Carmichael and Charles Hamilton:

> Black Power recognizes—it must recognize—the ethnic basis of American politics as well as the power-oriented nature of American politics. Black Power therefore calls for black people to consolidate behind their own, so that they can bargain from a position of strength. But while we endorse the *procedure* of group solidarity and identity for purpose of attaining certain goals in the body politic, this does not mean that black people should strive for the same kind of rewards (*i.e.*, end results) obtained by the white society. The ultimate values and goals are not domination or exploitation of other groups, but rather an effective share in the total

power of the society.[8]

Black Power in no way seeks to negate the humanity of whites. Rather it confronts whites with the reality that the values and traditions of power distribution in America have made whites incapable of accepting blacks as equals. Therefore, any change in white attitudes, *vis-à-vis* blacks, must be a direct result of black assertiveness in all spheres of life. The white man can only be free of his racism as he is forced to view blacks (using definitions of blacks and being confronted by blacks) as human, political and economic equals. Only when this becomes a reality will there be a demise of the subtleties of racism as manifested in white paternalism, ignorance and fear.

Black Power cannot guarantee to whites total nonviolent responses in the black man's quest for political and economic equality. Black people will use any means necessary to achieve full equality in a society founded on the ideal of the "inalienable rights of men." Whites must realize that Black Power is not predicated on violence or nonviolence but on the survival and full participation of blacks in the benefits of the American society. It is this dedication to the right of black people to survive that will determine whether black people will respond violently or nonviolently to racist forces. It is suicidal for black people in light of the legacy of violence committed against them by whites to accept nonviolent, purely "legal" tactics: "To expect . . . the [black] community to show neither anger nor hate, neither fear nor violence, when their values are challenged and their aspirations frustrated is to ask for the impossible."[9]

We are trying to understand the disillusionment and disenchantment of many blacks with white Christianity. In this respect Black Power functions as an ideological base of spiri-

---

[8] Carmichael and Hamilton, p. 47.
[9] Tannenbaum, p. 115.

tual awareness for those blacks who realize the spiritual dimension of their humanity but who cannot identify and intimately associate with what they conceive to be a white, blue-eyed Jesus—a Jesus who negates the humanity of their blackness, a Jesus who demands that they whiten their souls in order to save them.

Black Power as a subjective and objective force does not pretend to be able to meet the spiritual needs of blacks. But, as advocated and developed by individual blacks and black organizations, it does contain a body of impressions about what role religion ought to play in the life of the "new black man."

Black Power indicates to a black man that any experience with God, in light of one's everyday exploitation and persecution, is only real and beneficial if that God can actively empathize with him and act against those forces which seek to destroy him. Black Power indicates that God must be made over into an image and likeness consistent with redefined blackness: God must be able to deal with black children who are victimized daily by poor education, malnutrition, rats and roaches; a black man who has been unemployed for five years; a black mother whose young son recently died of lead poisoning from eating fallen paint in a dilapidated apartment; a young black student who senses the shame and hypocrisy of the so-called democratic ideals of the white world.

In reality God must become black. He must become the God not of "the sweet by and by" but of the bitter here and now.

Black Power provides the impetus which drives a black man to dictate *his terms of agreement* with any religion. There is developing within a substantial segment of the black community a distinct body of theology—Black Theology. The major goal of Black Theology is to redefine religion in terms which minimize its otherworldly and futuristic elements and to replace them with concern for daily needs and attempts of black people to assert their humanity and establish political and economic power. With this understanding, Black Theology is a continuing expression of an historical rejection of white Christianity on the part of many black people. It is in part a fulfillment of the need that Richard Allen and Absalom Jones felt for a religion that would recognize the human equality of blacks; in part a fulfillment of the need that Frederick Douglass felt for a religion that would identify with the needs of the oppressed poor; in part a fulfillment of the need that W. E. B. DuBois demanded for a religion that reflects its high creed of love and brotherhood in practical, concrete actions; in part a fulfillment of the need that Langston Hughes' Jesse B. Semple had for a religion which allowed him to relate to God without negating his blackness. In a very real sense, Black Theology asserts that God has become incarnate or immanent in such a way that he can relate to the needs of an oppressed black people.

As Julius Lester has said, God then becomes "the God of Nat Turner and Rap Brown, the God of Muddy Waters and B. B. King, the God of Aretha Franklin and the Impressions, this great God Almighty Everlasting *et in terra pax hominubus,* and all them other good things. . . ."[10]

One of the most significant expressions of Black Theology in the twentieth century is that of the Black Muslim movement under the leadership of the Honorable Elijah Muhammad.[11] Mr. Muhammad sensed in the late thirties the need of the black masses to redefine their religious experience independent of white racist "Christianity." He embraces and

[10] Julius Lester, *Black Folktales* (New York: Richard W. Baron, 1969), p. 130.
[11] See C. Eric Lincoln, *The Black Muslims in America* (Boston: Beacon Press, 1961); E. U. Essien-Udom, *Black Nationalism: A Search for an Identity in America* (New York: Dell Publishing Co., Inc., 1964); and Louis E. Lomax, *When the World Is Given* (Cleveland: World Publishing Co., 1963). The reader should also note that Black Theology in its early manifestation was developed by Marcus Garvey in the 1920's. See Marcus Garvey, *Philosophy of Opinions of Marcus Garvey,* 2 Vols. (New York: University Publishing House, 1923) and E. D. Cronon, *Black Moses* (Madison: University of Wisconsin Press, 1962).

develops a theology, which he believes to be consistent with the religion of Islam. The Black Muslims do not seek to restructure Christianity so that it provides a religious expression for blacks but to totally repudiate Christianity as a tool of oppression and as an ideology that perpetuates black powerlessness.

As indicated by Louis Lomax, the impact of this movement on the development of Black Theology and social protest is that the indictment of Christianity by the Black Muslims has "forced thoughtful Negro Preachers into an almost impossible position."[12] Lomax continues,

> I have talked this over with scores of Negro clergymen, and almost to a man, they agree that Muhammad has deeply shaken the Negro Christian community. Muhammad's recital of how the Christian faith has failed the Negro—"By their fruits ye shall know them"—has sunk deeper into the hearts of the Negro masses than Negro clergymen will admit publicly.[13]

Moreover—and this is the important point—"no gospel that fails to answer Muhammad's criticism of Christianity will be accepted. . . ."[14]

A particular and popular expression of Black Theology which does attempt to answer Muhammad's criticisms by reformulating Christianity has been developed by Albert Cleage of Central Church in Detroit, Michigan. He espouses a body of religious ideology which, in his thinking, restores blackness and truth to the history of ancient Israel, Jesus and Christianity.[15] For Cleage, blacks need not reject Christianity but a white, "honkified" perversion of it. Because Christianity has been twisted and distorted by racists, many blacks, ac-

---

[12] Louis E. Lomax, *The Negro Revolt* (New York: New American Library, 1962), p. 188.
[13] *Ibid.*
[14] *Ibid.*
[15] See his *Black Messiah* (New York: Sheed and Ward, 1968).

cording to his argument, have developed a white Jesus who sanctions and blesses the atrocities committed by whites against blacks. Cleage feels that it is crucial that the black identity of Jesus be exposed.

When I say that Jesus was black, that Jesus was the black Messiah, I'm not saying, "Wouldn't it be nice if Jesus was black?" or "Let's pretend that Jesus was black." I'm saying that Jesus WAS black. There never was a white Jesus. Now if you're white you can accept him if you want to, and you can go through psychological gymnastics and pretend that he was white, but he was black. If you're such a white racist that you've got to believe he was white, then you're going to distort history to preserve his whiteness.[16]

Cleage reconstructs a Jesus whose whole life was spent in challenging and seeking to destroy forces of racism represented by the white Roman power. He believes that black people today have a similar mission towards institutional racism by reordering and redefining their lives in order to gain an independent base of power.

Cleage's challenge to all blacks who desire an experience with Christianity is that they must repudiate a white Christ. Until they do so,

they have not freed themselves from their spiritual bondage to the white man nor established in their minds their right to first class citizenship in Christ's kingdom on earth. Black people cannot build dignity on their knees worshipping a white Christ. We must put down this white Jesus which the white man gave us in slavery and which has been tearing us to pieces.[17]

The emergence of Black Theology, especially as expressed by Albert Cleage, indicates very clearly the present disillu-

---

[16] Quoted in an important and widely circulated article in "The Quest for a Black Christ" in *Ebony,* March, 1969, p. 174.
[17] *Ibid.,* p. 176.

sionment and rejection by a significant number of blacks of a white Christianity. Black people by their rejection of Christianity are *by that very act* manifesting a search for the fulfillment of their spiritual needs.

In view of this a redefined black people must evaluate the truth and reality of Christianity independent of white racist definitions and expressions in institutions of oppression. Until blacks can objectively examine and assess Christianity and its Christ in this way, their minds are still being controlled by the white world. In effect failure to do this would contradict the positive forces of Black Power as we have described them.

It appears on the surface that Cleage and other black theologians have indeed redefined a Christianity independent from white thinking. But in reality they have only reconstructed a Christ and a Christianity after an image and likeness which is black. They have defined Christianity almost solely on the basis of color consciousness. It is still left to blacks to answer the question of whether or not there is something more substantive to Christ than his color and his ability to meet the need of black Americans who seek to acquire political and economic power in order to throw off every vestige of white domination.

Is the true nature of true Christianity ever ultimately dependent upon the expression of those who profess to be Christian? Is Christianity ever completely synonymous with human institutions? Is it possible for blacks and whites to have their spiritual needs met by one and the same God who affirms the humanity of both?

6
WHAT THE BLACK MAN MUST KNOW ABOUT CHRISTIANITY

We saw in the last chapter that Black Power enables blacks to redefine their existence and role in a white racist world. Black Power makes it possible for blacks to view themselves as men. It also confronts the white world with the reality of the humanity of blacks and therefore makes it possible for whites to be resensitized to their own humanity which has been obscured by the forces of white racism.

Black Power perceived in this way is the most creative and positive force operating in American society to bring the black world and the white world together. If America is to survive as a nation and to realize its high ideals of the human dignity and worth of all men and of their right to participate in a free society, Black Power must be recognized as a positive, not a destructive, force.

The greatness of America has always been tainted by its inability to express the equality and freedom of all of its people (especially its black people). Black Power enables both blacks and nonblacks to view themselves and each

79

other as human and equal citizens and thereby lays the basis for the necessary restructuring and reorganizing of American institutions which will actualize freedom and equality, not oppression and discrimination.

We have seen that Black Power also lays a basis and a desire for a new black religious experience and expression. Those religionists, who criticize and fear Black Power because of its implications of what religion should be for the new black man, fail to comprehend the potentially positive religious forces which Black Power precipitates.

Any person who hates himself has, in a very real sense, disqualified himself for an experience with God. Black Power seeks to destroy the negative self-concept and images (created in the white world and furthered by its institutions) that make black people hate themselves and view themselves as less than human. These negative concepts are replaced with a positive self-image which affirms the full humanity of blacks, the beauty of blackness, the rich legacy of black achievements and the potential of blacks in controlling their own destiny. A theological basis for their affirmation will be taken up later in this chapter. Here it is enough to say that a sense of independent responsibility and worth has a tendency to confront a man with his own adequacy and inadequacy, his own strengths and weaknesses and his own achievements and failures.

It is absurd to confront oppressed people with a sense of guilt and wrong when they, by definition, are the victims of hate and exploitation of others and view themselves as innocent and powerless victims of oppression. To tell a black man who is insensitive to his humanity that in order for him to have an experience with God he must confess his own guilt and wrong is, psychologically and historically, an insensitive display of religious creed.

Jesse B. Semple expressed the black man's inability to accept his personal guilt, sin and damnation by saying that he knows he is going to heaven because he has already been in the hell of Harlem. As long as an individual can project or displace his failure, apathy and social impotence to others, he is incapable of accepting full human responsibility, thereby disqualifying himself from a complete and genuine experience with God. The subjective force of Black Power emancipates a black man to accept the reality of *his* responsibility because he is human.

In addition to a sense of full human responsibility, the new black man has a new potential to objectively evaluate dominant issues that relate to his total humanity. Implicit in any evaluation of the black man's total humanity is a confrontation with his "spiritual" needs. It is, therefore, incumbent upon black people to re-evaluate "Christianity" which they have justifiably concluded is white, dehumanizing and oppressive. Throughout the black protest against the whiteness of Christianity, there were black men who consistently made the vital distinction between "Christianity" (as expressed and espoused by oppressors and their institutions) and Christianity (as an independent religious reality). Frederick Douglass concluded that his attack against Christianity, which we previously mentioned, was a charge against

> the *slave-holding religion* of this land, and with no possible reference to Christianity proper; for, between the Christianity of this land, and the Christianity of Christ, *I recognize the widest possible difference*—so wide, that to receive the one as good, pure, and holy, is of necessity to reject the other as bad, corrupt, and wicked. . . . I love the pure perceivable and impartial Christianity of Christ: I therefore hate the corrupt, slaveholding, women-whipping, cradle-plundering, partial and hypocritical Christianity of this land. Indeed, I can see no reason, but the most deceitful one, for calling the religion of this land Christianity. I look upon it as the climax of all misnomers, the boldest of all frauds, and

the grossest of all libels.[1]

Richard Allen and Absalom Jones, W. E. B. DuBois, Richard Wright, James Baldwin and Malcolm X all made the vital distinction between what Christianity is in its racist expression and what Christianity objectively is and ought to be to all who claim to be followers of Christ. Even Malcolm X in his *Autobiography* shows his awareness of the independent reality of true Christianity.

I would explain that it was our [the Muslims'] belief that Christianity did not perform what Christ taught. I never failed to cite that even Billy Graham, challenged in Africa, had himself made the distinction, "I believe in Christ, not Christianity."[2]

An awareness of this distinction between what Christianity *is* and how Christianity *was used* in America against blacks enables us to conclude that the truth of Christianity cannot be determined solely by its sociological expression in American history. There is reason for suspicion and hostility on the part of blacks; this has been demonstrated. But both the non-Christian black man and white man who desire to judge Christianity must ask the elemental question: What is true Christianity and how do I know it is true?

The black man who wants to think independently cannot allow the white "Christian" society, which has lied about and lied to blacks, to define the Christian faith for him. The white American who has perverted history to exclude his own atrocities and the black man's achievements also may have perverted Christianity.

Those blacks who reject the Christian God as too white and inseparably united to racist ideology and institutions must have this image destroyed if they are to have an experience with the *true* God. We have come to believe that the

---

[1] Frederick Douglass, *Narrative of the Life of Frederick Douglass: An American Slave,* Signet Books (New York: New American Library, 1968), p. 120.
[2] Malcolm X, p. 286.

true God who can meet the total objective and subjective needs of all people is the God manifested in the historical person of Jesus Christ.

This realization in no way seeks to distract from and offset the fact that black people have an unimpeachable case against white "Christianity." But it is meant to emphasize that black people like all other people in our society will never ultimately be satisfied and truly free until they have had a genuine redemptive experience with God who has made himself known in Jesus Christ.

We have shown that Black Power is a positive force operating among blacks in that it resensitizes them to their humanity and responsibility and allows them to objectively evaluate and deal with forces operating in their everyday world. However, Black Power, as we have described it, is not intended and designed to meet the specific "spiritual" need for a right standing before a holy and loving God that is common to all men.

Because of the negative impressions prevalent among a significant number of blacks concerning the ability of "Christianity" to meet this need, every independent-thinking black person must examine the original source of the Christian religion and then determine whether or not his need for a right standing with God is met by the Christian God—not the white God of racist "Christianity."

A black man in quest of God must learn from other blacks who are disillusioned with "Christianity" yet recognize that its relevance and truth cannot be determined by such indirect sociological analyses. To discover what real Christianity teaches one must go back to the "primary sources." This is analogous, for example, to discovering the real truth about the Black Muslims or the Black Panthers: One examines the "primary sources"—their holy books, their formative statements of philosophy, ethics, belief and their promotional materials.

In approaching Christianity one must thoroughly scruti-
nize the Bible to determine what it actually teaches about the
black man and his relationship to God and other men.

If a black man accepts the distinction between an ideology
and the use of that ideology, he can understand how the
Bible was misused and distorted to justify the inhuman treatment of blacks by whites. In addition, if it can be demonstrated that the white man's use of the Bible to justify his
racism is spurious, then every free-thinking black ought to
evaluate the Bible independently—free from white intimida-
tion—as it pertains to race *and* to other universal aspects of
the human dilemma.

The first chapter of this book demonstrated that the major
foundation for the support of slavery and white supremacy
was the biblical record of the "curse on Ham" erroneously
interpreted as a curse on blacks. We also saw that the Bible
was interpreted by many whites to sanction the "natural
order" of the slave institution and that Paul's teaching concerning slave-master relations was construed and presented so
as to justify slavery and to foster a docility that was a necessary attribute of the "perfect slave." We would like to consider what in fact the Bible *does say* about each of these
teachings.

Genesis 9:18-27 has been used by many white racists for
years to teach that black people have been cursed by God to
be in utter subjection and slavery to the nonblack "races."
The biblical incident involves Noah, his three sons (Japheth,
Ham and Shem) and one of his grandsons, Canaan, the
youngest son of Ham. After the flood, Noah planted a vine-
yard and became drunk from its wine. In his tent he lay
uncovered and his son Ham saw Noah's nakedness and told
his two brothers, Shem and Japheth. These two sons took a
robe and walked in backwards so that they would not see
their father's nakedness and covered the drunken Noah.

When Noah awoke and learned what had happened he

spoke these words, "Cursed be Canaan; a slave of slaves shall he be to his brothers." Noah continued his prophecy with a comment about each son, repeating twice that Canaan is to be a slave to his brothers.

It is obvious from this passage that the curse pronounced by Noah is *not* upon Ham but upon Canaan. Therefore, in order to reconstruct what took place, whatever sinful act occurred and elicited Noah's curse, it cannot be ascribed to Ham, but to Canaan. The apparent contradiction between the fact that the text records that Ham saw "the nakedness of his father" and the fact that Canaan is cursed by Noah is adequately explained by an alternate meaning of "youngest son" in verse 24. It records that "when Noah awoke from his wine and knew what his youngest son had done to him," he pronounced the curse upon Canaan. But since Ham is not Noah's youngest son, the guilty party was another. The alternate meaning of "youngest son" is "grandson" which in this case would logically explain why the curse is upon Canaan, the grandson of Noah.[3]

Thus having established that Canaan and not Ham was the object of Noah's curse, it remains to be seen how the incident has been twisted to apply to blacks. In order to apply "the curse" to blacks these propositions must be taught in the text: (1) Blacks are descendents of Canaan, (2) Noah's words are valid *as a curse*, (3) the curse applies today and (4) we should enforce the curse.

None of these are supported clearly by the teaching of the passage and the first is even strongly contradicted. The pronouncement, which is best understood as a *prophecy*, is not applied to Ham but to Canaan, Ham's youngest son, and thus it only could be applied to Canaan's descendents. The progeny of Canaan are recorded in Genesis 10:15-19, and it is

---

[3] Silberman, p. 174. We do not feel that it is wise to speculate upon Canaan's impropriety, yet the fact remains that Canaan, not Ham, was both the "guilty" and the "cursed" individual.

clear that they are *not* inhabitants of Africa and were not considered as black-skinned by those of the ancient world.[4] The exegetical fact that blacks are not descendents of Canaan is enough to refute the arguments that Noah's prophecy applies to black people today. In addition, the prophecy seems to have been fulfilled through the defeat of the Canaanites by the children of Israel as recorded in the book of Joshua. This victory, ordained by God as a judgment for sin, subdued the Canaanites who were not killed (cf. Joshua 9:23 in regard to the Gibeonites). Thus if the curse is to be fulfilled today it would apply to a small number of white descendents of Canaan who have not intermarried with descendents of Shem and Japheth. The Bible does not teach that black people are cursed by God to an inferior status but rather predicts judgment on the white Canaanites for their sins.

It should also be noted that the Bible does actually record in Genesis 10 the contributions of those who are the indisputable progenitors of blacks. To Ham's other sons, Cush, Egypt and Put, are ascribed the earliest beginnings of great human civilizations, such as Assyria, Babylon, Accad, Egypt and Ethiopia.[5] In this respect the Bible demonstrates its honesty and objectivity in recording the accomplishments and history of all ancient people.

Color distinctions to justify a man's dominance over another man are basically the fruits of a racist mind. God as revealed in the Bible is not governed by distinctions of color. But our purposes in exposing the "colors" of Canaan and Ham's other descendents is to show black people, who live in

---

[4] William F. Albright, "The Old Testament World," *The Interpreter's Bible* (New York: Abingdon Press, 1952), I, 270.

[5] Genesis 10:6-14. DuBois in *The World and Africa,* chaps. 5-6, corroborates the *blackness* of these ancient kingdoms. See also J. C. deGraft-Johnson, *African Glory* (New York: Walker and Company, 1954); Harry R. Hall, *Ancient History of the Near East,* 11th ed. (New York: Barnes and Noble, 1960); and Harry R. Johnston, *A History of the Colonization of Africa by Alien Races* (New York: Cooper Square, 1966).

a color-conscious world, the absolute objectivity and integrity of a book which has been mishandled and misrepresented by white oppressors.

The Bible, the original source of Christian teaching, neither teaches nor supports the inhuman institution of slavery, especially in its barbarous American form.

The first argument adduced to defend slavery was that slavery is a "natural" expression of God's will to introduce "illiterate," "uncivilized" blacks to the benefits of white western civilization. This type of "theological" reasoning is absurd as a defense of slavery (or segregation). For example, it is "natural" that corrupt men seeking gain for themselves organize crime syndicates and provide a great source of enjoyment and release from frustration to a great mass of people. God has *allowed* it, but that does not mean that he has *approved* it. This type of argument in defense of slavery or segregation fails to distinguish between what God approves and what God allows. God permits events to accomplish his will, but all that he permits is not according to his desires. God's providential will (*i.e.*, what actually happens) does not equal his desired will. Slavery, therefore, cannot be attributed to the desired will of God, but to man's evil desire to dominate another for his own gain.

A second type of proslavery argument is based upon biblical examples of both slavery and segregation. The tirades, "What God approved in the Old Testament and sanctioned in the New, cannot be sin," notwithstanding, these examples do not support American slavery or segregation. If everything which the Bible reports and God permitted was to be an example for us to follow, then polygamy, murder and divorce are God's express will for men today.[6] Jesus' words in Matthew 19:8 to the effect that Moses allowed divorce because of man's sinful nature illustrate this principle. There

---

[6] Consider Jacob and his two wives Leah and Rachel, the actions of Israel in conquering Canaan and the bill of divorcement provision in Deuteronomy 24:1-4.

were provisions in the Old Testament for divorce but Jesus says divorce is not part of God's desired will, because the principles of God's original intent in creation are against it. Likewise, because there are examples of slavery in the Bible and provisions for certain aspects of it does not mean that slavery is God's will.

The third supposed biblical support for slavery and, indirectly, for segregation is the New Testament instructions for slaves and masters.[7] Since most of these passages were written by the Apostle Paul, he has been subjected to various verbal assaults and his teachings have been interpreted to serve as the basis for a repudiation of Christianity. If Paul's teaching is to be properly understood, the following points must be considered: (1) Paul was not dealing with slavery identical to American chattel racial slavery, (2) Paul dealt only with relations between slave and master *within* the Christian community, not *outside*, (3) Paul's very instructions actually undermined the whole institution of slavery and (4) Paul espoused a body of teaching which would make it *impossible* for Christians ever to institute or initiate a slavery system.

First, slavery in the Roman world of Paul's day was not founded upon a supposed superiority or inferiority of people *based on the color of their skin*. A person's servitude did not indicate his innate human worth and capabilities. Usually one became a slave because of forces of circumstance or fate, such as defeat in war or economic deprivations. The slave in the Roman world had rights and privileges which were not afforded to slaves in the United States, *e.g.*, rights of family, legal recourse against masters, rights of private ownership and access to manumission without permanent stigma.[8] (Our allu-

---

[7]Cf. Titus 2:9-10, Ephesians 6:5-9, Colossians 3:22-25, 1 Peter 2:18-25 and 1 Timothy 6:1-2.

[8]Cf. William L. Westermann, *Slave Systems of Greek and Roman Antiquity* (Philadelphia: American Philosophical Society, 1955). The reader is also encouraged to compare the similarities between Latin American and Roman slavery,

sion to these rights and privileges is not meant to justify slavery *in any form* but only to highlight the contrasts between the Roman and American types.) All too often it has been assumed that slavery in the Roman world was exclusively limited to blacks. This explains why racist minds could easily use Pauline passages to justify their treatment of blacks in America. However, slavery in ancient Rome was not limited to any single ethnic group or class. It was possible for any man or woman to become a slave.

Second, Paul addressed himself only to those masters and slaves who had received his message and become Christians. The principles which he set forth are not meant to govern the larger society on the issue of slavery. These principles neither abrogate nor set aside the privileges which a slave, Christian or not, had before Roman law. Thus if Pauline teaching regarding the obedience of slaves is to be applied to all blacks, then all blacks must by definition be Christians, and that runs counter to the assumptions on which missions to blacks were based and which are indeed patently false.

Third, it is a historical fact that the principles which Paul taught concerning slave-master relations within the Christian community actually laid the foundation for the abolition of slavery in the Roman world.[9] Paul's principles, if examined closely, will show that the relation between master and slave is based on human equality and mutual respect which are by nature incompatible with slavery. Moreover, since in the Roman world slavery was basically a machinery for social and economic organization, Paul's statement that masters should give to their slaves that which is "just and equal" would make it impossible for slavery to continue as a viable, profitable institution.[10]

---

both of which contrast with slavery in the United States. See Tannenbaum, *passim.*

[9] *Ibid.*

[10] Colossians 4:1 (KJV).

WHAT THE BLACK MAN MUST KNOW ABOUT CHRISTIANITY

Fourth, many who criticize Paul because he did not condemn slavery as it had manifested itself in chattel, racial slavery in America fail to realize that he could not condemn that which did not exist. Paul does teach principles which would condemn any who would initiate or create slave institutions and who, at the same time, call themselves Christians. This statement is not meant to judge or condemn all those in the past who called themselves Christians and held slaves; but it is only meant to suggest that one has reason to suspect their true character.

The revolutionary concepts of man's unity and worth based upon God's act of creation made all men brothers. In addition, the realistic teaching of Paul that all men are by nature evil and capable of atrocious domination of others is a strong principle that argues for the eradication of slavery. Paul further teaches that in the Christian community racial, social and class distinctions are of no importance: "There is neither Jew nor Greek, there is neither slave nor free, there is neither male nor female; for you are all one in Christ Jesus."[11]

Having exposed the false nature of white racist thought in their use of the Bible to justify the exploitation of blacks in America, we can conclude that there is no such thing as a biblical curse on blacks as descendents of Ham and no biblical basis to support the slave institution. If indeed a redefined black man is capable of thinking independently of racist definitions and teachings, he must confess that the Bible must not be rejected as a book which gives whites license to subjugate blacks. He will concede that the objectivity and honesty of the Bible in relationship to black people has been demonstrated. What then does the Bible teach positively about blacks (and mankind in general) in relation to God?

The Bible teaches that the universe and all within it has come into being by the will and action of a personal, triune

[11]Galatians 3:28.

God. The God of both the Old and New Testaments is the sovereign Creator-God who in the beginning created the heavens and the earth *ex nihilo*. The Psalmist sang the praises of the creator and stood in awe at his power.

Praise the Lord!
Praise the Lord from the heavens,
    praise him in the heights!
Praise him, all his angels,
    praise him, all his host!

Praise him, sun and moon,
    praise him, all you shining stars!
Praise him, you highest heavens,
    and you waters above the heavens!

Let them praise the name of the Lord!
    For he commanded and they were created.
And he established them for ever and ever;
    he fixed their bounds which cannot be passed.[12]

The prophets of the Old Testament likewise declared the reality of God as creator.[13] Jesus, the self-confessed God-Man, assumed God as creator when he spoke of God as the all-loving Father who providentially controlled the most insignificant aspects of the world.[14] At the end of the biblical canon the heavens cry in praise to God the Creator:

Worthy art thou, our Lord and God,
    to receive glory and honor and power
for thou didst create all things,
    and by thy will they existed and were created.[15]

The meaning of the doctrine of creation, particularly as it is applied to the black man in America today, centers in the

---

[12] Psalm 148:1-6.
[13] Isaiah 40:25-29; Amos 4:13.
[14] Cf. Luke 12:7, Matthew 10:2ff and 5:47-48.
[15] Revelation 4:11.

biblical affirmation that "God saw everything that he had made, and behold, it was very good."[16] For the individual who knows the Creator-God, human existence is not meaningless. Despite the frustrations and evil of daily life, the creation itself and its movement in history is under the control of God's purpose. Creation should not be understood as a surreptitious attempt to countenance gradualism or to condone injustice. Rather it is a recognition of the basis for *meaning* in life for all men, black and white.

Man is at the focal point in God's creation. He is not a mere creature like others but is uniquely created by the direct activity of God. The Bible records that "God created man in his own image . . ."[17] and that "the Lord God formed man of dust from the ground, and breathed into his nostrils the breath of life; and man became a living being."[18] Thus God created man as an animated body like all other living beings, *but in God's own image*. This is not a white image or a black image. Man is a "psycho-physical unity: both a body *and* a soul, completely and simultaneously."[19]

The fact that man is created in the image and likeness of God gives man the full potential and privilege of having intimate communion with the God who created him. Yet because of this "image of God" in man, no man can be fully satisfied until he experiences the reality of this personal relationship with God.

The most obvious application of the biblical teaching concerning the creation of man is that all men have equal value and dignity. God created one pair of humans from whom all men and women derive. They are all equally in the image of God because mankind is a unity—from a common source,

---

[16]Genesis 1:31a.
[17]Genesis 1:27.
[18]Genesis 2:7.
[19]Stuart Barton Babbage, *Man in Nature and in Grace* (Grand Rapids: William B. Eerdmans, 1957), p. 11.

Adam. The importance of this should not be overlooked because "the decision to promote equality of opportunity in the social order is an ethical decision and does not stand or fall according to whether scientists furnish indisputable proof that biological equality exists."[20] As an ethical decision, equality of treatment must have a legitimate basis. Christian doctrine provides a basis, relating equality directly to God's creative activity.

In addition to affirming the unity of humanity the biblical teaching concerning the creation of man also supports the worth of the individual and his right to survive as an expression of creation. The individual must recognize that *he* is worthy of respect and dignity and possesses the right of survival. We have seen that Black Power as a positive psychological force among many blacks *asserts* the reality of the dignity and worth of blacks and of their right to survive. But it cannot be said to *support* it. The creation of man in the image and likeness of God becomes the support for this reality.

Perhaps one of the most beautiful expressions of the meaning of the creation of man is found in this adaptation from the Talmud:

Why did God create only one Adam and not many at a time?

He did this to demonstrate that one man in himself is an entire universe. Also He wished to teach mankind that he who kills one human being is as guilty as if he had destroyed the entire world. Similarly, he who saves the life of one single human being is as worthy as if he had saved all humanity.

God created only one man so that people should not try to feel superior to one another and boast of their lineage in this wise: "I am descended from a more dis-

---

[20]Leona E. Tyler, *The Psychology of Human Differences,* 3d ed. (New York: Appleton-Century-Crofts, 1965), p. 304.

tinguished Adam than you."

He also did this so that the heathen should not be able to say that since many men had been created at the same time, it was conclusive proof that there was more than one God.

Lastly, He did this in order to establish His own power and glory. When a maker of coins does his work he uses only one mould and all the coins emerge alike. But the King of Kings, blessed be His Name, has created all mankind in the mould of Adam, and even so no man is identical to another. For this reason each person must respect himself and say with dignity: "God created the world on my account. Therefore, let me not lose eternal life because of some vain passion!"[21]

The Bible records the rebellion of man through the sin of Adam which broke fellowship between God and man. It teaches that each individual born since that rebellious act has inherited the evil nature of his predecessor, Adam, and thus by nature rebels and revolts against the will of his God-Creator. The penalty for this revolt is death—separation from God—which climaxes in "the punishment of eternal destruction and exclusion from the presence of the Lord and from the glory of his might."[22]

God, however, has acted graciously toward man by doing for man what man could not do for himself. God himself became man and though he partook of human nature he did so apart from sin. "The Word became flesh" (John 1:14) and shared the struggles of humanity. Jesus Christ, the eternal Son of God, "knew himself to be a man" and suffered temptation, weariness, hunger and thirst and all the joys and sorrows of common humanity. "His whole manner of life was

[21]Quoted in Edmund Fuller, *Affirmations of God and Man: Writings for Modern Dialogue* (New York: Association Press, 1967), pp. 48-49.
[22]2 Thessalonians 1:9.

genuinely human."²³ Yet he was God come "in the likeness of sinful flesh [humanity], and for sin, condemned sin in the flesh [his body]"²⁴ in order to bring forgiveness to all men who turn to him in repentance and trust. When God became Man, he entered the world as the son of a poor family living in a despised and persecuted nation. He did not identify himself with earthly royalty and riches, though he was King of Kings, but identified himself with humility and poverty.

The character of God as revealed in the earthly life of the God-Man, Jesus Christ, displays qualities which speak to the modern tensions existing between blacks and whites. Jesus revealed the character of God by word and deed.

A primary theme of his teaching was the Kingdom of God. By this he did not mean simply an earthly, secular kingdom which would be like the nations of the earth. Rather he stressed that the Kingdom was realized as God's rule in the lives of men who submitted themselves to him. This Kingdom finds its present expression *within history*, in the lives of those who submit to God's will, and its full and future expression in the earthly reign of the King himself who returns to establish it.

Although there are these futuristic aspects to the Kingdom, the present realities of God's power and love were to be manifested in the lives of those who accepted Christ's *present* kingly rule. This present aspect of the Kingdom of God thus affirms the dignity, value and right to survival of all men, either as actual or as potential members of that kingdom. It is not an act of socio-political suicide for any man to submit his life to Christ as Lord and Savior.

In this connection we must clarify an important point. The popular understanding of Jesus' principle of "turning the

---

²³Leon Morris, *The Lord from Heaven: A Study of the New Testament Teaching on the Deity and Humanity of Jesus Christ* (Grand Rapids: William B. Eerdmans, 1958), p. 45.
²⁴Romans 8:3 (KJV).

other cheek" implying that a Christian simply acquiesces to forces of harm and destruction is, in our thinking, erroneous. One must distinguish between suffering for righteousness' sake (by virtue of identification with Christ) and suffering because of man's inhumanity to man.

We believe the former does make it necessary for one who is a Christian to "turn the other cheek" when persecuted as a Christian, but the latter makes it incumbent upon *every man*, created in the image of God, to actively resist forces that threaten his survival.

But, since the turn-the-other-cheek principle has been misused and misinterpreted by many "Christians" to justify the totally nonviolent response of black people to institutions of oppression, many blacks have come to view Christianity as incompatible with black survival in its fullest sense. This is blasphemy!

Black people, like all other people in society, have operating within the deepest levels of their personalities the principle of survival that originates from God himself. The same principle that operates when any white man protects himself and his family from a burglar with a drawn gun makes it necessary for blacks to respond to white police brutality in ways which will enable them to survive. This principle means that a black man whose family is being harassed by white mobs will respond in ways which protect his own well being and that of his family. This principle means that black parents who recognize the inequities of an educational system which teaches their young will respond in ways which eliminate these inequities.

The guiding principle of life for those who consider themselves members of Christ's present Kingdom (*i.e.*, those who consider themselves to be Christians) consists of loving obedience to God and loving concern for other men. Jesus himself summed up the revealed will of God in these two great commandments:

You shall love the Lord your God with all your heart,
and with all your soul, and with all your mind. This is
the great and first commandment. And a second is like
it, You shall love your neighbor as yourself.[25]
These commandments, which only Jesus has perfectly fulfilled, obviously exclude all elements of racism and discrimination.

Not only did Jesus' teaching concerning the ethic of the
Kingdom of God challenge bigotry and prejudice, but his
actions did likewise. One of the most despised "racial"
groups of New Testament times were Samaritans. It was the
Jewish people who expressed their hatred and disregard for
them because the Samaritans, though "half-Jewish," were
religious schismatics. Jesus, while recognizing their religious
errors, did not despise them. Jesus while travelling through
Samaria met an adulterous woman at Jacob's well.[26] He
spoke with her because he recognized her dignity as a person
created by God. Jesus kindly led her to see her need of
spiritual life and to comprehend his own identity as the Sent
One of God.

One of Jesus' most famous parables, the Good Samaritan,
is a damning indictment of the hypocrisy and bigotry of his
contemporaries. The one who proved himself neighbor was
not the Jewish priest or the Levite but the Samaritan. The
Samaritan, whom Jesus' countrymen despised, was the only
one who showed mercy to the injured man despite sacrifice
on his own part. The neighbor-love which Jesus taught is not
limited by societal bigotry and prejudices.[27]

The supreme action of Jesus Christ demonstrating his repudiation of racism and discrimination was his self-sacrificial
crucifixion for the guilt of the world. Indeed, the whole pur-

[25] Matthew 22:37-39.
[26] John 4:1-30.
[27] Paul Ramsey, *Basic Christian Ethics* (New York: Charles Scribner's Sons,
1950), pp. 92ff.

pose of God becoming Man and sharing man's suffering was to die for the selfishness, bigotry, discrimination, inhumanity and rebellion of *all* men who would put their trust in him, regardless of their economic, political, social or racial status. His death on the cross is applicable on equal terms of faith and repentance to all men. Jesus said that he "came not to be served but to serve, and to give his life as a ransom [payment for sin] for many [people]."[28] That those people were to be from all nations and races of the world is clear from Jesus' command to his apostles to "Go therefore and make disciples of all nations. . . ."[29]

On the basis of the universal redemption in Jesus Christ, any group that calls itself *Christian* and discriminates against a race or class is simply rejecting the biblical, Christian pattern. The New Testament church was not composed of nice, ticky-tacky, middle-class people.[30] Rather, the unity of faith overcame the potential divisions of social and racial barriers which were everywhere present. The meek and mild, white, Nordic Jesus is phony—at best a product of ignorant ethnocentrism, at worst of white racism.[31] Jesus is not the God of white people; he is the God of the universe and his death for the rebellion of this world applies to people of all races.

If one desires to be a Christian, he must personally trust Jesus Christ as Savior from personal sin and he must personally commit himself to Christ as Lord in his daily life. Christianity is Christ—Christ who has died, risen and ascended into heaven to provide full forgiveness and power to those who

---

[28] Mark 10:45.

[29] Matthew 28:19a.

[30] The color of Jesus in our thinking is totally irrelevant to that which he came to accomplish and that which he demonstrated. We do not find in his life any attitudes which would suggest that a man must give up his blackness or whiteness in order to become a Christian. If one wants to consider the color of Jesus using racist criteria (*i.e.,* "one drop of black blood makes you black"), then Jesus *is* black.

[31] 1 Corinthians 6:9-11, James 2:1-7, Acts 16:25-34, *et al.*

follow him. Black Power as a subjective psychological force can never give the individual the completeness of life and wholeness of personality that is available in the reality of acceptance and fellowship with God as revealed in Jesus Christ.

We have seen in this chapter several vital factors that must ultimately govern an individual's response to Christianity. An independent-thinking black (or anyone) must first consider the positive religious functions of Black Power in that (1) it provides a sense of responsibility and (2) it demands a thinking independent of racist patterns and, therefore, drives a man to objectivity and honesty in evaluating the true nature of Christianity.

Second, he must recognize that true Christianity is to be distinguished from its sociological expression with its racist attitudes and actions. The Bible is the ultimate authority and source to determine what Christianity is.

Third, the Bible itself does not support in any way the subjugation of blacks by whites. The curse on Ham to justify white oppression does not exist; the black slave experience in America cannot be attributed to God's desired will.

Fourth, the Bible teaches the full human equality and worth of all men as created in the image of God. This equality and worth was most supremely manifested when the self-confessed God-Man, Jesus Christ, offered his life to bring forgiveness to all who trust in him, regardless of their racial or social status. Moreover, the individual who commits himself to Christ as the God who provides forgiveness and fullness of life does not negate his identity nor abdicate his right to survival in a hostile environment.

Therefore any black man who now rejects the Christ of true Christianity *cannot* reject him because of his "whiteness" and his supposed association with forces of oppression. Rather, any rejection of Jesus Christ can only be based upon a black individual's refusal to accept a Christ who challenges him with his own human inadequacies, failures and guilt. And this rejection is none other than a refusal to accept a "redefined" Jesus who is willing and able to enter into the struggle of black people in white America.

7

WHAT THE WHITE CHRISTIAN MUST DO WITH HIS CHURCH

Despite the emphasis in the last chapter, we do not believe that the racial crisis in America will be automatically solved by blacks alone. A positive response by redefined blacks to true Christianity is not enough.

Racism in America is basically a white problem: White society created it and keeps it going through its institutions. If institutions reflect the attitudes and values of its people, then the most ideal and humane way for whites to eliminate institutional racism is for them to change their attitudes about blacks, restructuring and reorganizing their institutions so that they no longer oppress, but liberate and provide equal opportunity for all citizens.[1]

Whites must begin to view blacks as human beings en-

---

[1] While it appears to us that the most effective solution to racism is attitudinal change leading to structural (institutional) change, the deep-seated nature of white racism makes it imperative that in some cases structural change precede attitudinal change if oppression of blacks is to be quickly and effectively eliminated.

dowed with the same rights and privileges as white people. Nonetheless, our discussion of Black Power has demonstrated the inability of whites to make this change apart from black assertiveness and confrontation.

In this chapter we would like to suggest ways in which the white Christian community, both individually and corporately, can act in order for greater justice and equality to be realized and for the black man's negative impressions of Christianity to be altered.

We have demonstrated that "Christianity" has been and continues for the most part to be inextricably bound to racist institutions. "The white church as an institution has not only been supported by but has also *given its sanction to* the other major institutions of the society—business, education, and government."[2] It cannot be too strongly emphasized that Christianity as an institution (regardless of theological refinements or denominational distinctions) has been the major force in undergirding and approving the values of the sociopolitical and economic institutions of America. Peter Berger in analyzing the relationship of Christianity to American institutions concludes that "commitment to Christianity . . . undergoes a fatal identification with commitment to society, to respectability, to the American way of life."[3]

Just as the white church has supported and continues to support oppressive forces by both its action and inaction, we believe that the white church, recognizing its true identity as God's people who should function as a force for good, can generate and advance those values which liberate and promote justice for all Americans. The inability of the white Christian church to demonstrate values which oppose racist forces has cancelled the church as a viable force in aiding

---

[2] Lewis M. Killian, *The Impossible Revolution? Black Power and the American Dream* (New York: Random House, 1968), p. 23.

[3] Peter Berger, *The Noise of Solemn Assemblies* (New York: Doubleday and Co., 1961), p. 116.

black people (and others) in their quest for survival.

We hesitate to offer pre-packaged programs to the racial crisis because of a realistic awareness of the everchanging milieu in which racism must be attacked. Today's solutions may become tomorrow's problems. Only active, daily involvement can be fruitful in judging the feasibility of any proposed solution.

To those who insist upon detailed and concrete plans of action, . . . [we] can only urgently advise them to consult their congressman, their psychoanalyst, or better still, if they are determined believers, their local priest. . . . [We] can take this facetious method of answering with a good conscience because . . . [we are] convinced that we all, deep in our hearts, *know exactly what to do*, though most of us would rather die than do it.[4]

Because racism is a multiheaded monster, its destruction demands a diversity of responses, programs and solutions. The individual who commits himself to the abolition of racism must deal initially with his own racist attitudes and fears. If he doesn't, he will merely help further racism, not abolish it.

First, anyone who calls himself Christian (in the biblical sense) must *repent* of any attitudes that would give him a sense of superiority in respect to another man.[5] The beginning of the elimination of white racism is the admission of guilt: the admission that I am wrong, that I have offended, that I have benefited from a society that assumes my superiority because I am white and the black man's inferiority because he is black.

A white man who says, "I never owned slaves," or "I never raped a black woman," or "I did not kill Emmett Till," or "I did not bomb the four black girls in Alabama," or "I have

---

[4] Richard Wright, *White Man, Listen!* (New York: Doubleday and Co., Inc., 1964), p. xvi, italics ours.

[5] James 2:8-9, 2 Corinthians 7:8-10, 1 John 1:9-10.

not opposed open housing," is escaping a confrontation with his own guilt. His guilt is the guilt of ignorance, the guilt of insensitivity to the cry and the struggle of black people, the guilt of omission which refuses to stop the continual oppression and domination of blacks by whites.

> What white Americans have never fully understood—but what . . . [blacks] can never forget—is that the white society is deeply implicated in the ghetto [the epitome of the oppression of blacks]. White institutions created it, white institutions maintain it, and white society condones it.[6]

This full admission of guilt does not in any way destroy the reality of a white man's humanity. Part of the white racist mental pathology is that whites cannot admit their guilt in oppressing blacks because in their thinking a "superior people" can do no wrong. Because of this, many whites often view slavery as a benign introduction of blacks to the benefits of Western civilization. They also view segregation and subordination as desirable to blacks.

We believe, however, that the white man who admits his ignorance and guilt and confronts his fears is, in actuality, *affirming* his humanity, because he views himself as a creature capable of both good and evil. Still, this realization should not be viewed as an "if-then" argument. That is, whites cannot escape their own guilt by saying that blacks, being human, would have done the same thing if they had had the opportunity.

The fact is that *whites have created and maintained* institutions which commit atrocities against blacks for which all whites (either directly or indirectly, consciously or unconsciously) share a responsibility.

The present day black reparation demands of James Forman and others manifest concretely a black awareness of

---

[6] *Report of the National Advisory Commission on Civil Disorders*, p. 2.

the complicity and conjunction of institutional Christianity (which is obviously white dominated) with the various forms of institutional racism. But the demand for reparations from white Christian churches is, in our opinion, but one of a myriad of black initiatives against white Christian racist institutions. No given amount of money paid by white Christian churches to blacks can compensate for the atrocities committed by white Christianity. The payment of reparations is too easy an option for whites to exercise to remove their guilt about "the black problem" and to minimize their personal involvement—especially when one considers that white Christian churches participate in and significantly benefit from the greatest economy the world has ever known. Still, many white church bodies try to meet reparation demands by simply giving the monetary crumbs of their real wealth.

While reparation payments may be one proper response, the complexity of white racism and its effects, as abetted by the forces of Christianity, demands that white Christians not only give their money but their own lives to help restructure our society. Forceful action must take place on all levels, not simply to erase guilt but to revamp American society so that blacks can participate as political, economic and human equals. In addition, blacks will not simply wait for white churches to respond to their reparation demands but will continue to initiate in all areas those programs and policies which will give blacks actual power bases.[7]

The authors have met many whites who have cried and wept as they have admitted their own racism but who have not truly repented: Their actions (or lack of them) betray the change which they claim to have had. The last group that will help eradicate racism in America are whites who simply weep

---

[7] Reparations, as frequently presented, are not concerned with whether or not Christianity is a workable religion for blacks, but reparations are rather primarily concerned with the reality that Christianity *must pay* for its crimes against black people.

and wail about their guilt. A change of attitude, based upon the admission of guilt must, in order to be valid, issue in change of action. Specifically, in whatever ways necessary whites must actively support blacks in their survival struggle against institutional racism as manifested in housing, employment and other forms of discrimination.

Some Christians do not feel that they or their churches should be involved in the socio-political problems created by white racism. Many believe that social concern will divert the church from its mission—evangelism. Admittedly, the message of the Kingdom of God must be spread so that men can come to a personal relationship with God. They believe and practice Jesus' words that "repentance and forgiveness of sins should be preached in his name to all nations."[8] Anything, they say, which competes with or diverts from preaching the Good News of Jesus Christ is categorically wrong.

But this objection is founded on the false assumption that Christians may *either* preach the Good News *or* work to improve social conditions. This is a false dichotomy: It is not a matter of either/or, but both/and. Jesus did not endorse a dichotomy between physical and spiritual ministries. The first chapter of the Gospel according to Mark records that the activities of Jesus, apparently in the same day, included teaching in the synagogue, casting out evil spirits and in late evening healing many sick. The compassion of Jesus moved him to minister to the whole man. Christians, who must be like Jesus, should not separate spiritual and social needs. Just as "works without faith is dead," so "faith without works is dead."

Since God commands Christians to "do good to all men"[9] and to be "careful to apply themselves to good deeds,"[10] then we are disobedient Christians if we do not evidence

---
[8] Luke 24:47.
[9] Galatians 6:10.
[10] Titus 3:8.

social concern which issues in overt action. The Great Commission itself commands to "make disciples . . . teaching them to observe all that I have commanded you." [11] And the teaching of Jesus includes that children of the Kingdom should be perfect as their heavenly Father is perfect, who does good to all men and sends sun and rain upon the evil and the good. [12]

Christians should therefore be taught to *do* those actions which promote the good of all men. Christians should act on behalf of justice and righteousness in the social and political spheres and *not* neglect proclaiming salvation through the reconciling death of the God-Man, Jesus Christ. The example of Christ means that Christians must be involved in ministering to the whole man. It is totally inconceivable for a Christian to say that he loves men if he does not attack those forces which destroy men themselves.

Others object that attempts to solve social problems are futile because, by nature, social problems are insoluble. This, however, is not a genuine objection to Christian involvement with social problems and social change since no one assumes that the problems can be finally and completely solved. In the light of this fact, further illuminated by the biblical insight concerning the sinfulness of human nature, Christian social action must be absolutely realistic. But if social evils will never be completely removed in this age, it does not follow that they cannot or should not be minimized *as much as possible*. [13] The Christian church is not responsible for success; it is responsible for obedience to the will of God who desires righteousness and justice in social, political and economic affairs.

White Christians often object: "You can't legislate love.

---

[11] Matthew 28:19-20.
[12] Matthew 5:43-48.
[13] Cf. Paul's statements in 1 Timothy 4:1 and 6:11 in which Timothy is exhorted to work for righteousness despite growing evil.

White people will be prejudiced against blacks no matter how many laws are passed." But the goal of Christian social action is not to make people love one another but to stop them from expressing their hatred in overt individual and institutional ways that oppress other people. Penalties for murder do not eliminate the evil desire to murder, but they may discourage the act. Likewise, legal measures taken against racial discrimination attempt to change the action, not the attitude. In addition recent studies have shown that *law does change attitude*. Thus the very objection is clearly false.[14]

A final objection to Christian social action is that it compromises the Christian faith. That is to say, the Christian faith is necessarily compromised when it cooperates in an endeavor with non-Christians. But this objection fails to take into account the fact that such cooperation takes place every day without compromise of the Christian faith. Christians drive on the right side of the road, just like non-Christians; Christians pay taxes, just like non-Christians; and they write letters to congressmen, vote for the President, and register their dogs, just like non-Christians, and in mutual agreement with non-Christians.

The issue of cooperation with non-Christians really concerns the *level* of cooperation. Most Christians believe that it would be wrong to cooperate religiously with non-Christians as if there were no differences between them. The Bible teaches that that is indeed correct.[15] But in matters of common interest which do not involve necessary endorsement of a common religious position, the Bible indicates that we can

---

[14]John R. Roche and Milton M. Gordon, "Can Morality Be Legislated?" in *American Minorities: A Textbook of Readings in Intergroup Relations,* ed. by Milton L. Barron (New York: Alfred A. Knopf, 1958), pp. 490-96. These authors conclude that although local considerations may call for special forms of implementation, "the majesty of law, when supported by the collective conscience of a people and the healing power of the social situation, in the long run will not only enforce morality but create it" (p. 496).
[15] 2 Corinthians 6:14—7:1.

and sometimes *should* cooperate with non-Christians.[16]

Conflict no doubt will arise, and perhaps there will be frictions because of the Good News of Jesus Christ. But these are not reasons for non-involvement. In fact, non-involvement or so-called neutrality *is* a social position. It "conveys, implicitly, an endorsement of the status quo. It puts one into the position of seeming to bless or sanctify evil leaders, institutions, and practices instead of exposing and condemning the works of evil."[17] Neutrality also implies that the message of the church is "totally irrelevant to practical problems except, perhaps, as it might change the motivations and aspirations of individuals who respond to it."[18]

Therefore, in light of biblical support for Christian involvement in the total society on behalf of the good of the *whole* man, we believe that it is the proper mission of the Christian church to actively support leadership and programs working (1) to destroy the forces of institutional racism and (2) to create a society in which the justice of God is realized in the institutions of men.

This active support may take on many forms. In one instance financial support may be primary, *e.g.*, money for the building of black community enterprises; in another instance, an individual Christian or organization of Christians may join in active cooperation with the program of others, *e.g.*, local pressure groups for black inclusion in trade unions and local educational control; in another instance, Christians may provide leadership to programs which seek to promote racial justice and harmony, *e.g.*, educating *whites* in the larger society at *all* levels concerning the need for social and attitudinal change.

---

[16]For example see Romans 13:1-7, 1 Corinthians 5:9-13 and Jesus' statement in John 17:15 that Christians are *in* this world.

[17]David O. Moberg, *Inasmuch: Christian Social Responsibility in 20th Century America* (Grand Rapids: William B. Eerdmans, 1965), p. 14.

[18]*Ibid.*

The ability of the Christian church as a major institutional force in accomplishing this kind of social change should not be minimized. The historical role of Christianity has been indicated as the primary force determining the normative values of our society—a society which is manifestly racist. If Christian institutions were used effectively to support racist values and institutions, how much more should they now effectively support and create values and institutions which recognize the dignity and equality of all races?

The white Christian church which has realized its responsibility to work actively to destroy racism often does not recognize that the very inner structure of its own church may maintain policies and attitudes that contribute to the very racism it seeks to destroy. Just as we noted in Chapter Three that the racism of the total society today has taken on a subtle and evasive form in respect to its oppression of blacks, so the racism of the white church is difficult to fully isolate and identify. However, as one focuses upon the inner structures of the white Christian church, he can see features, programs and attitudes which are racist.

For example, the curricula of the white church, with few exceptions, represent the world as all white. They tell the receivers of their messages and images that all that is significant in this world and the world to come is white. It would appear to the church members that God lives in suburbs, fights crab grass, has middle-class values and is white. These attitudes, impressions and values when transferred to the larger society would lead the individual to believe that God is not concerned with the everyday oppression of blacks and that the ghettos are the products of black ignorance, laziness and immorality.

Another way in which the inner structure of the white church perpetuates racism is by investing and spending its monies and resources oftentimes with enterprises which directly or indirectly exploit the black community or which deny blacks equal opportunity in employment, housing and education. White church organizations and leadership have also unofficially supported national and local political leadership that has been identified with conservative and gradualistic policies in relation to the solution of race problems.

But probably the greatest support that the white church gives to racist institutions is its lack of commitment to black organizations which are trying to alleviate the oppression of blacks. For example, it appears that the policy of most white churches is not to speak out against the savage murder and beatings of black people by policemen; not to use their influence to change deplorable housing conditions; or not to use their influence to change the "whiteness" of their local school curriculum.

Yet another evidence of racism within the white church is the overwhelming tendency to flee when blacks move into the neighborhood. The justifications given usually camouflage the real reason for the flight: the fear of black men having sex relations with white women.

Experience shows that white Christians share this common fear with the larger white world. The reader will recall that during slavery blacks were totally dependent on whites. Because of this, whites began to look at blacks as objects of utility. Blacks, stripped of their humanity, were reduced to the animal level. It is precisely at this point that we find a perversion in the white male's sexual outlook on the black male and female. Many white men had elevated white women to the level of purity and super-chastity, and began to have unrestricted sexual relationships with black women who could not resist their advances because of the power these white men wielded in a society they controlled.

Whites have always respected the right of a white man to protect his wife and daughters from sexual advances. Realizing that black men had the same protective responses toward their women, the white man began to imagine that black men were obsessed with the desire to retaliate. The white man translated this obsession as a black male's desire for sex relationships with his own most precious possession— his pure, white woman.

This could not help but lead to the fantastic exaggeration in the white man's mind of the Negro male's sexual prowess. And this, in turn, would necessitate more repressive measures against the Negro male—all caused by the white man's guilt and anxiety. The necessity to "protect" the white female against this fancied prowess of the male Negro thus became a fixed constellation in the ethos of the South.[19]

These sexual fears and mythologies are not the sole expression of Southern whites, but indeed extend throughout all of the strata of white society—North and South. The sexual basis for white racism in America cannot be neglected: ". . . In the core of the heart of the American race problem the sex factor is rooted; rooted so deeply that it is not always recognized when it shows at the surface."[20]

Physical proximity with blacks, in the thinking of many whites, produces the condition in which black men can act out this supposed obsession.[21] A current illustration of this from personal experience involves a white community's response to enforced school desegregation in a Southern town. A news reporter related to one of the authors the fact that white mothers were seeking birth control information to prevent having children, for such children would have contact

[19]Kardiner and Ovesey, p. 45.
[20]J. W. Johnson, *Along This Way* (New York: Viking Press, 1933), p. 170.
[21]We believe that, because of racist ideology and myths created by the white community seeking to justify its sexual exploits among blacks both in and out of slavery, there are some black men and women who do desire sexual relations with whites and vice versa. A casual observation, however, of the physical characteristics of so-called black people in America would indicate that white men should be held more in suspicion concerning sexual activity with black women, than black men with white women. Cf. Calvin Herton, *Sex and Racism in America* (New York: Grove Press, Inc., 1965); and Grier and Cobbs.

that might lead to interracial sex relations. Though this is an extreme example, the fact is that such attitudes do more to prevent whites from having permanent involvement with blacks on an equal basis than any other set of racist attitudes.

Eldridge Cleaver presents a lucid perspective on the dominant white male's sexual barriers to true racial equality. Cleaver constructs an address of a white male to a black male:

> I [the white male] will have access to the white woman and I will have access to the black woman. The black woman will have access to you—but she will also have access to me. I forbid you access to the white woman. The white woman will have access to me, the Omnipotent Administrator, but I deny her access to you, you the Supermasculine Menial. By subjecting your manhood to the control of my will, I shall control. The stem of the Body, the penis, must submit to the will of the Brain.[22]

It is tragic that such fears and perversions run rampant, both consciously and unconsciously, among white people, even those who claim to be followers of Christ.

The authors recognize that the "logical" extension of these fears is in the prohibition of interracial marriages which in the Western world has been almost exclusively limited to considerations of color. There is no biblical basis to support such restrictions. The only biblical restriction on marriage is that a man marry a woman and a woman a man.

Yet another evidence of white racism in the white church is the refusal of white Christians to accept a black leadership which will not compromise with racism in any form and which challenges the status quo. Most white churches will pick and support black-skinned individuals (Negroes) who are least threatening to the church's real position on social issues

[22] Eldridge Cleaver, *Soul on Ice* (New York: McGraw-Hill Book Company, 1968), p. 165.

relative to race. The white church which has come to view Black Power as a positive force in America cannot afford to delude itself in selecting black leadership. It can only properly *recognize* black leadership!

Though admittedly we have not isolated all the manifestations of attitudinal and structural racism within the white Christian church, we believe that those aspects which we have named provide adequate opportunities for white involvement in the elimination of white racism.

To those white Christians who invariably ask, "What can we do?" we say without equivocation, "De-honkify (de-whiten) your church: its curriculum, its investment and purchasing programs, its leadership and its attitudes."

This type of action will not and cannot be a passive, gradual program. The racist attitudes and actions of the Christian church must be forcefully attacked, producing vigorous confrontation that should result in the eventual desired structural and attitudinal changes. James Baldwin says it so well: "The subtle and deadly change of heart that might occur in you would be involved with the realization that a civilization is not destroyed by wicked people: it is not necessary that people be wicked but only that they be spineless." Only a genuine, active social involvement will afford the white Christian church the opportunity to become that positive sociological expression of Christianity which will aid the black man in his re-evaluation and assessment of the true person and work of Jesus Christ.

To those white Christians who would ask for more concrete instruction on what to do, we would reiterate Richard Wright's words: "We all, deep in our hearts, *know exactly what to do*, though most of us would rather die than do it."